100 DIARIES

THAT CHRONICLED WORLD EVENTS

machten

Ich … will

werden! Aber

mehr, als ein

daß Arbeiter

System

Schöpfung, vom

ist in der Reg

Das

etwas einfa

hoffe ich

Pavilion
An imprint of HarperCollinsPublishers Ltd
1 London Bridge Street
London SE1 9GF

www.harpercollins.co.uk

HarperCollinsPublishers
Macken House
39/40 Mayor Street Upper,
Dublin 1
D01 C9W8
Ireland

10 9 8 7 6 5 4 3 2 1

First published in Great Britain by Pavilion
An imprint of HarperCollinsPublishers 2025

ISBN 9780008562106

Publishing Director: Laura Russell
Editor: Shamar Gunning
Editorial Assistant: Daisy Gudmunsen
Design Manager: Alice Kennedy-Owen
Layout Designer: Cara Rogers
Production Controller: Emma Hatlen
Proofreader: Kathy Woolley
Indexer: Vanessa Bird

Printed and bound by Papercraft in Malaysia

100 DIARIES
THAT CHRONICLED WORLD EVENTS

COLIN SALTER

PAVILION

DAS TAGEBUCH

DER

ANNE FRANK

14. Juni 1942 - 1. August 1944

Das Tagebuch zeichnet ein Bild der täglichen Hölle, aber auch eines der prallen Schönheit des Lebens. Kein Dichter unserer Zeit hat das Zwielicht unserer Situation, die sinnbildlich für uns alle genommen werden kann, so echt und ursprünglich schildern können wie dieses vierzehnjährige Mädchen, das sein armes, einsames und verängstigtes Leben dann doch noch, kurz vor Kriegsende, in Bergen-Belsen beendete. Das Buch hat wenig mit »Politik« zu tun und viel mit dem Menschen unserer Tage. Es geht nicht um ein zufälliges Schicksal einer Familie, es geht um ein gültiges Dokument, das stellvertretend für alle steht, und das, bitter-süßes Geschenk, uns von einem Kinde geschaffen worden ist.

»Deutsche Kommentare«

VERLAG LAMBERT SCHNEIDER · HEIDELBERG

ABOVE: *The first German edition of* Das Tagebuch der Anne Frank *or* The Diary of Anne Frank, *published in Heidelberg, Germany in 1950.* *(see page 204)*

Contents

ABOVE: Samuel Pepys, in a wood engraving from 1849, surrounded by his papers and writing what we can presume to be his diary. *(see page 36)*

Introduction

Dear diary ...

Thousands of diaries survive from history – voices from the past with something to tell us about their lives and times. But why should we listen?

Some diaries have come down to us despite their authors' requests that they be burned after their deaths – Virginia Woolf's is one example. Others were written in code to prevent readers from discovering the truth about their authors such as the journal of Yorkshire landowner Anne Lister who did not want her family to know about her private life. Many were hidden to prevent the wrong eyes seeing them such as that of Petter Moen, a Norwegian resistance fighter in World War Two, who knew that he would be punished, and his diary destroyed if it were ever found by the Nazis.

Other diaries have been written expressly in order to be read later, even if only by the author – Virginia Woolf (again) wrote to her future self in the knowledge that her diaries would be the basis of a memoir. Jakob Walter, a foot soldier in the Napoleonic Wars, kept a diary of its horrors which he later presented to his son (not yet born at his time of writing) as evidence of what he had survived.

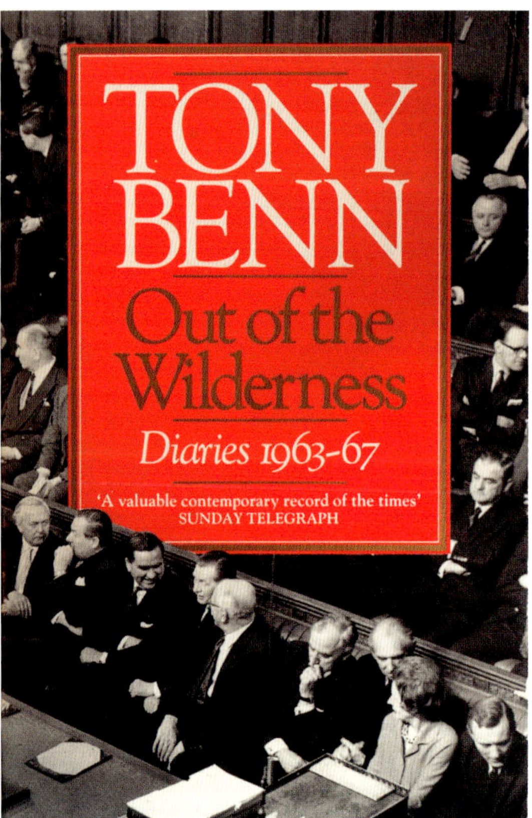

PROFESSIONAL AND PERSONAL

Some diaries are kept purely as official records – accounts by emperors, queens and presidents can be included here. Although these may have begun as formal accounts of decisions and appointments in office, nevertheless the personality and life of the diarist still leaks out in, for example, young Queen Victoria's memories of her coronation, or the delight of Japan's Emperor Uda in his cat.

Others offer chilling insights into their authors' characters – Heinrich Himmler could report an execution order of hundreds of Jews as dispassionately as he could note arrangements for dinner the same evening. The two boys who carried out the Columbine High School massacre in 1999 both kept diaries which chart their journey from social outcasts to murderers.

Diaries are personal. Diaries from the past are the personal witness to a history which is not recorded in the deeds, contracts, treaties and accounts of nations. President Truman's diary records not only his meetings with world leaders like Winston Churchill and Josef

LEFT: Tony Benn's published diaries gives modern readers an insight into the British political climate of the 1960s. *(see page 196)*

Stalin but his personal view of the terrible power of the atomic bomb whose use he authorised. Those on the ground in Hiroshima however had a different perspective, such as that recounted in the Hiroshima diary by Dr. Michihiko, an eyewitness to the event. The same of course is true of all victims of war, far from the minds of those conducting the war from positions of power. Anne Frank is the obvious example; and sadly many other such diaries were written at the time. The awful choices facing Adam Czerniaków, the head of the Jewish Council in the Warsaw Ghetto, pose the same ethical dilemmas today that they did in 1942.

DIFFERENT POINT OF VIEW

Diaries allow us to see the world through other people's eyes. Even in the twenty-first century, when we can see everything everywhere on personal screens, our travels are capable of surprising us with new cultures and different ways of doing things. We do not have to travel so very far back in time to find diarists for whom the sights and sounds of new places were extraordinary. The French absurdist author Albert Camus's impressions of New York, to which he travelled just after World War Two, are a delightful voyage of personal discovery. At the other end of history, Christopher Columbus – the first European to "discover" America – brought a very different set of prejudices to bear on his assessment of the New World.

American historians are blessed with many journals which record the nation's relatively short history through the eyes of settlers like Nicholas Cresswell. Non-settlers too – visitors from Europe – began to see differences between two societies with so much common cultural baggage. Janet Schaw, arriving from Scotland on the eve of the American War of Independence, was very disapproving of the practices she found in North Carolina, and decided not to settle there after all.

With many journals which record the nation's relatively short history through the eyes of settlers like Nicholas Cresswell. Non-settlers too – visitors from Europe – began to see differences between two societies

RIGHT: Hiroshima Diary *by Dr. Michihiko gives readers a harrowing eyewitness account of one of the greatest atrocities in modern history.*

with so much common cultural baggage. Janet Schaw, arriving from Scotland on the eve of the American War of Independence, was very disapproving of the practices which she found in North Carolina, and decided not to settle there after all.

Other travellers in historic lands have similar tales to tell. Choe Bu, a fifteenth-century Korean official, was shipwrecked on the shores of China and kept an invaluable diary of the journey as he made his way back to Korea overland through the cultures of the varied Chinese landscape. Joseph Jenkins fled to Australia to escape his murderous wife in Wales, and his outsider's observations of nineteenth-century Australian colonial life are now a standard text in Australian schools.

BELOW: An inscribed copy of MAGICK in Theory and Practice *by The Master Therion (Aleister Crowley).* *(see page 140)*

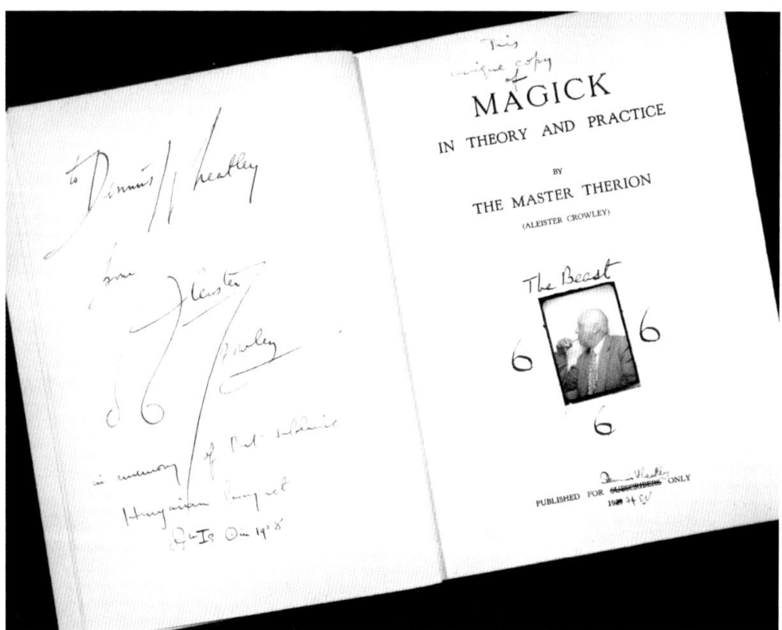

NOTEBOOKS AS SKETCHBOOKS

'It strikes me,' Virginia Woolf once observed, 'that in this book I practise writing; do my scales.' Woolf used her diary as a notebook to clarify the future ideas of her novels and many diarists have used their journals in similar ways. Ralph Waldo Emerson based many of his lectures (and subsequent books) on the musings in his diaries. Composer Richard Wagner marked the progress of his next work in his diary; and the great American novelist John Steinbeck kept a diary especially to observe his work practices over the five months it took to write The Grapes of Wrath.

For some, diary writing is a religious practice. Maria Heyde was a German missionary in Tibet whose devotion to her faith and to the population which she served, under frequent hardship for nearly fifty years, reflects through her writing. A religion of a very different kind was practiced by the occultist Aleister Crowley, who developed his philosophy 'Do what thou wilt shall be the whole of the Law' and his own religion, Thelema, in the pages of his diaries and encouraged his acolytes to chart their own spiritual progress in the same way.

Writing an idea down gives it a shape, a form of words; and often it is only when diarists see that shape that they understand the idea's strengths and weaknesses. This is as true for the philosopher Henry David Thoreau as it is for Nella Last, a British housewife. Mrs Last, who lived through World War Two and kept one of the longest diaries in the English language was an ordinary, compassionate wife and mother. Her journal contains illustrative examples of the impact of "big" history on "little" people; yet one of the greatest pleasures of reading it is the development of her own ideas of herself. Without the diary, which she began after an appeal from a social sciences project, Mrs Last would never have discovered her gift for writing, which she became aware of only through her entries. This gave Nella a sense of self-worth – which, in turn, opened her eyes to the everyday sexism of her husband and others. Hers is a diary which revealed as much to her as it does to us.

TELLING THE TRUTH

At times, diaries can play the role of confessor. Fifteenth-century diarist Gregorio Dati was a Florentine merchant; and alongside the day's accounts he would confess its temptations and sins. Samuel Pepys, one of the most famous diarists in the English language, frequently admitted his faults and indiscretions in the pages of his diary, although – it must be said – with little regret.

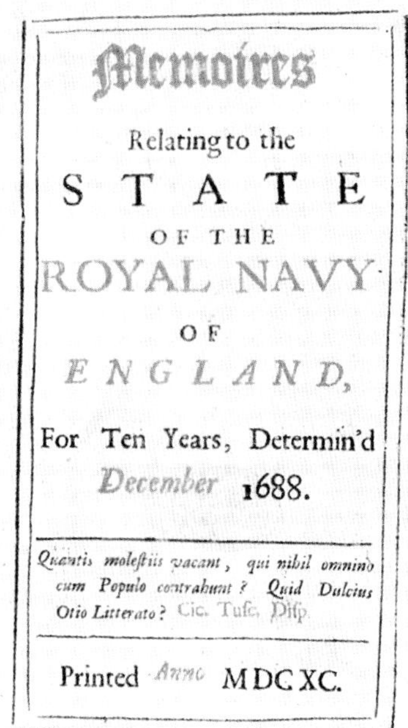

Memoires
Relating to the
STATE
OF THE
ROYAL NAVY
OF
ENGLAND,
For Ten Years, Determin'd
December 1688.

Quantis molestiis vacant, qui nihil omnino cum Populo contrahunt? Quid Dulcius Otio Litterato? Cic. Tusc. Disp.

Printed Anno MDCXC.

ABOVE: The Diary of Samuel Pepys, *candidly admits to his own misgivings, alongside one of the most definitive accounts of this period in British history.* *(see page 36)*

Emily Pepys, no relation to Samuel, was a mischievous Scottish schoolgirl who often felt obliged, more by her teacher than her conscience, to record her nineteenth-century misbehaviour. The journal of her Russian counterpart Nina Sergeyevna Lugovskaya, written a century later, shows that teenagers are teenagers regardless of when they were born. Both pages are filled with morbid anxieties, an obsession with the opposite sex and a lack of respect for authority (which for one growing up in Stalinist Russia had serious consequences).

Do remember that diaries are unreliable histories. Diarists leave things out all the time: either because they are not important to the writer; because they are too important to risk being discovered; because the diarist is simply unaware of them; disapproves of them, or is too distressed by them to allow their thoughts to take shape on the page. Still, diaries add vital colour to the grey tapestry of "factual" history and they bring it to life for readers. Every single one of us makes a contribution to history through our decisions and our lifestyles, both mundane and impactful.

A diary need not cover a lifetime in order to have impact. Nor does it need the lifetime be a long one in order to move us. History is composed of individual moments and turning points which, like a diary, may only make sense afterwards when read together.

We *are* the life in the history of our times; and so in the pages of this book you will find diaries not only of the famous and powerful – artists, revolutionaries, rulers and discoverers – but those from every level of society, in every age, on every continent, who thought it worth writing down what they saw, suffered, enjoyed and observed in the world, large or small, around them.

Whether you keep your own diary, read those of others, or simply enjoy meeting new people, the hundred diaries in this volume are guaranteed to illuminate human history and introduce new characters. Enjoy reading – and perhaps, writing.

Emperor Uda, Japanese ruler

(866-931)

The oldest surviving diary in Japan was kept by its fifty-ninth emperor, a man of strong social and religious convictions – and a particular fondness for his cat. His diaries reveal a sensitive man in whom affairs of state competed with the small pleasures of everyday life.

Uda succeeded his father, Emperor Kōkō, in 887. Kōkō had been on the throne for only three years when he died at the age of fifty-six and Uda, Kōkō's third son, had not expected to succeed him. Writing in his diary in 889, Uda recalled 'shaking with fear' at his father's enthronement, an elaborate demonstration of power. He revealed, in an entry headlined 'A dream denied', that he had set his heart, when he was seventeen, of becoming a Buddhist monk. Uda was only twenty-one when he became emperor.

Uda's diary records both his official and his personal life. It was a celebrated historical document in the fourteenth century; but some of the ten sections known to have existed at that time were lost during a fifteenth-century war. Scholars have been able to reconstruct some of the missing fragments, thanks to secondary references in the works of those who consulted Uda's diary in the Middle Ages. What survives today was written between 887 and 890.

Uda had his political hands full with fending off the imperial claims of the powerful Fujiwara clan – Uda was of the Minamoto clan and used his power to post enemies in remote areas of the Japanese Empire. At home he appears to have been a just ruler. The Emperor ordered an amnesty for prisoners wrongly convicted of crimes and introduced a law preventing noble families from encroaching onto peasant land. Uda sought a return to traditional values within the imperial court, reviving an interest in the works and ethics of Confucius, in an attempt to reconcile his imperial duties with his Buddhist ambitions.

The most famous of his diary entries was an entirely personal one made on March 11th 889, under the heading 'For the Love of a Cat'. The cat in question was a gift from his late father five years earlier, and in Uda's eyes it outshone other felines in every respect. 'The pupils of his eyes sparkle,' Uda wrote, 'dazzlingly bright like shiny needles flashing with light'. Uda's admiration for the cat was positively poetic as he espoused, 'my cat moves silently, making not a single sound, like a black dragon above the clouds'.

Uda had no doubts about the (unnamed) cat's spiritual strength, the result of a Taoist diet: the cat 'instinctively follows the "five-bird' regimen"' and 'is good at catching mice at night, better at it than other cats'. And of course, like all pet owners, Uda talked to his cat. 'I once said to the cat, "You possess the forces of yin and yang and have a body that is the way it should be. I suspect that in your heart you may even know all about me!" The cat heaved a sigh, raised his head, and stared fixedly at my face, seeming so choked with emotion, his heart so full of feeling, that he could not say a thing in reply.'

Eventually, the tension between his profound Buddhist principles and the demands of empire became too much. Uda abdicated in favour of his eldest son in 897, when he was only thirty-one; and three years later he entered a monastery, where he remained for the rest of his life. History does not record whether, or not, the cat remained with him.

LEFT: A portrait of Emperor Uda, the 59th Emperor of Japan.

Lady Nijō, Japanese noblewoman

(1258-1307)

Lady Nijō was a concubine in the Japanese imperial court and her diaries are an often shocking record of her affairs and of the secrets she sometimes had to keep. One is tempted to wonder at times if she intended them for publication, or for blackmail.

Nijō wrote her diary in her late forties, over the course of three years, from 1304 to 1307. The entries describe the courtly antics of her life from 1271, when she was thirteen, to Nijō's present day. She was regarded as promiscuous by other concubines of the court, but she shrugged off their criticism, secure in the knowledge that she did what she had to do to survive. She was, by her own account, a very beautiful woman and understood her own small degree of power within a man's world.

Emperor Go-Fukakusa was in love with Lady Nijō's mother, who died soon after Nijō's birth; and in the hopes of currying favour, Lady Nijō's father gave her to the emperor as a concubine when Nijō was fourteen. Her father died only a year later, leaving Nijō without influence or protection in a court where, with the right backing, she might have aspired to be the Empress.

Nijō slept not only with the Emperor but with his brother Ariake (a Buddhist monk) and with a government minister named Akebono. Like many of us today, it seems she wrote her diaries to give her life some sense of meaningfulness. Nijō called her diary 'an unsolicited tale', and had little confidence that it would be of any worth; even noting, 'that all my dreams might not prove empty, I have been writing this useless account — though I doubt it will long survive me.'

She bore the Emperor one son, who died in infancy, and bore at least three other children from other lovers, who naturally had to be kept secret from Go-Fukakusa. Her poignant record of the birth of one of these children is one of the diaries' most moving passages.

'[Akebono] lit a lamp to look at the child, and I got a glimpse of fine black hair and eyes already opened. It was my own child, and naturally enough I thought it was adorable. As I looked on, [he] took the white gown beside me and wrapped the baby in it, cut the umbilical cord with a short sword that lay by my pillow, and taking the baby, left without a word to anyone. I did not even get a second glimpse of the child's face.

I wanted to cry out and ask why, if the baby must be taken away, I could not at least look at it again; but that would have been rash, and so I remained quiet, letting the tears on my sleeves express my feelings. "It will be all right. You have nothing to worry about. If it lives you'll be able to see it," Akebono said on his return, attempting to console me. Yet I could not forget the face I had glimpsed but once. Though it was only a girl, I was grieved to think that I did not even know where she had been taken. I also knew it would have been impossible to keep her even if I had so desired. There was nothing for me to do but wrap my sleeves around myself and sob inwardly.'

Lady Nijō was expelled from court in 1283 by a jealous courtesan of the Emperor and became an itinerant Buddhist nun. Her diary was lost for centuries until a copy was found in the imperial archives in 1940. Now published as Confessions of Lady Nijō, it tells the story of a fiercely proud, intelligent, literate woman in a world of men.

ABOVE: An eighteenth century sketch depicting two Japanese women. "Nijo" was not the diarist's true name, however the term "Nijō" denotes her position within the Japanese court.

Quatro gran fiumi et ben nauiughosi
rigan leterre dequesta partita
chentutte lescripture son famosi
detre fimroua donde anno salita
ilquarto uiene dapaesi focosi
et riga lenopia et a luscita
nelmar degipto et chiamasi ilcaligine
et gion et nilo et nonsi sa lorrigine
Frison e laltro molto alloriente
chedemonti dipersia alindia uersa
enuerso lostrecho a lacorrente
Tigris elterzo chesta sua trauersa
contro ghassiri et ua molto repente
eufrates e ilquarto elqual somersa
lacque sue incauerne et fa ritorno
et luno et laltro corre amezo giorno

Questi due escono degli monti ermini
doue poso dopo ildiluuio larcha
etutti atre fanno lunghi camini
insino chenelmar dindia ciaschun uarcha
elqual mare par chestenda suo confini
uenendo stretto dallocceana marcha
fino inarabia presso adsinay
giu uer ponente ad bassara et chessi
Quiui uengono dellindia editiopia
lemolte spetierie adquella gente
che uanno persse quando nanno inopia
perconducerle uerso locidente
quiui neuiene una incredibil copia
percorrouanne et successiuamente
mandano insieme dicamegli gran mandria
che portano adomascho et alessandria

ABOVE: Manuscript pages from La Sfera, circa 1450, by Gregorio Dati, including a hand-coloured map.

Gregorio Dati, merchant of Florence

(1363–1435)

Medieval Italian merchants routinely kept both public and private accounts of their personal and commercial dealings – one for the taxman, one for themselves. Gregorio Dati's 'Secret Book', as he called it, reveals the eternal struggle between serving God and making a profit.

Gregorio Dati was a silk merchant, trading in a product which was costly to produce and to sell. Merchants like him bought in the raw material of silk thread and paid weavers to turn it into cloth. As the cloth took several months to produce, weavers expected to receive part of their wage in advance, which put a financial strain on merchants.

Dati's father had been a wool merchant, and Florentine dealers preferred the more consistent quality of woollen cloth. Silk had a more individual finish depending on the merchant's taste and the weavers' ability, which made it harder for dealers to find the right market. As a result, many silk merchants relied on a more direct approach to their customers. Dati had to fund sailings to the better market at Valencia, and pay his brother who lived there to act as a dealer on his behalf.

On one trip which Dati himself made to Valencia in 1390, he recorded in his diary that the voyage would not be covered by the business and that he had failed to recoup a large debt – 400 Barcelona pounds – from one client. Attempting another trip, in 1393, Dati was kidnapped by pirates from Naples and held to ransom. A year later his business had to find another ransom sum for his brother who had been captured by the King of Anjou.

Despite such setbacks Dati was a relatively successful merchant. He courted the custom of popes and kings for whom expensive silk cloth was an affordable luxury; and at the age of sixty-four he was among the top 10% of wealthy Florentines. His personal life was more chaotic: he was married four times and the father of twenty-six children. All four of his wives died in pregnancy or childbirth; and only seven of his offspring survived him. Dati was a god-fearing man, instilled through his Catholic upbringing with a great sense of guilt and sin.

After the death of each of his children, he routinely wrote in his diaries that he hoped they would intercede on his behalf with the Virgin Mary in the expectation of forgiveness. On January 1st 1404, at the age of forty, he wrote down his resolutions for the coming year. They reveal the continuing tension between being a good Christian and making his business pay.

'I resolve from this day forward to refrain from going to the shop or conducting business on solemn Church holidays, or from permitting others to work for me or seek temporal gain on such days.

I resolve from this very day and in perpetuity to keep Friday as a day of total chastity – with Friday I include the following night – when I must abstain from the enjoyment of all carnal pleasures.

I resolve this day to do a third thing while I am in health and able to, remembering that each day we need Almighty God to provide for us. Each day I wish to honour God by some giving of alms or by the recitation of prayers or some other pious act.

I have written this down so that I might remember my promise and be ashamed if I should chance to break it.'

Does any of this sound familiar to twenty-first century makers of New Year Resolutions?

Christopher Columbus, Italian explorer

(1451 – 1506)

Christopher Columbus, often considered the discoverer of North America, kept a detailed journal of the first voyage, which he made between 1492 and 1493. His diary entries were distorted by the need to impress his sponsors, from whom he hoped to gain funding for further journeys.

Christopher Columbus, an Italian by birth, was paid by Queen Isabella of Spain not to discover a continent but to find a trade route by sea to the rich resources of India and the East Indies. Isabella was not the first person Columbus approached with his theory of the existence of such a passage: he already had rejection letters from John II of Portugal, Henry VII of England and the rulers of Venice, Genoa and France. Even Isabella turned him down once, before he managed to persuade her.

There was no such route approaching India from the east. Instead, Columbus made landfall in what he named the West Indies; and he found that someone was indeed already there. As an old teaching song goes:

So tell me, who discovered what?
He thought he was in a different spot.
Columbus was lost, the Caribs were not;
They were already here.

After nearly two months at sea Columbus, with his three ships the Santa Maria, the Niña and the Pinta, first came ashore on an island which he called San Salvador. This was probably the island in the Bahamas known for three centuries as Watling's Island, after the Englishman who claimed it in the seventeenth century, which was only renamed San Salvador in 1926. Columbus remained in the area for five months, exploring the Caribbean Sea including San Domingo and Cuba, and recording the people and natural resources which he found there.

He wrote his diary entries from a particular perspective, intended to stress the potential wealth of the West Indies to Queen Isabella in the hope that she would sponsor further expeditions. Emphasis was therefore placed on the ease with which a Spanish mission might conquer the islands: 'They neither carry nor know anything of arms,' he wrote on October 11th 1492, 'for I showed them swords, and they took them by the blade and cut themselves through ignorance.' He stressed, three days later, that 'with fifty men they can all be subjugated and made to do what is required of them'.

Columbus reckoned that two great incentives would convince Isabella to pay for further voyages: gold, and Christianity. 'I believe that they would easily be made Christians,' he noted, 'as it appeared to me that they had no religion'. But gold was the great prize, and Columbus was alert to any suggestion of its presence. 'I saw that some of them had a small piece fastened in a hole they have in the nose,' he observed, 'and by signs I was able to make out that to the south, or going from the island to the south, there was a king who had great cups full, and who possessed a great quantity'. Gold however seemed to hold little fascination for the islanders themselves.

This first meeting between southern Europeans and Caribbeans was the beginning of Europe's long plunder of the Americas and their peoples, driven by the idea that Europe was superior. Columbus noted after his first meeting with the islanders that 'they should be good servants and intelligent, for I observed that they quickly took in what was said to them'.

ABOVE: A portrait from 1719 of Christopher Colombus by the Italian painter and his contemporary Sebastiano del Piombo.

Choe Bu, Korean official and traveller

(1454–1504)

In an age when travel by sea was considerably easier and safer than travelling by land, court official Choe Bu kept a diary of his homeward journey through China after a shipwreck on a hostile shore. The resulting journal is a valuable outsider's view of life in the country during the Ming Dynasty.

Choe Bu was a career civil servant in the Korean government who worked his way up from a post in the National Library to great responsibility as a high-ranking official in the Directorate of Ceremonies. He was broadly educated in Chinese philosophy, poetry and literature at a time when Korea and China were considered to be on a cultural par. He contributed to the compilation of an exhaustive chronicle of Korea from the dawn of history to the present in 1485, which brought his literary skills to the attention of Korea's King Seongjong.

Choe Bu was dispatched in 1487 to Jeju, a large island off the southern tip of the Korean peninsula, with orders to account for runaway slaves who might have escaped there from the mainland. Early 1488 however he received news that his father had died, and set sail for home to mourn for him. During the crossing, a winter storm arose which threw the ship wildly off course and lasted for fourteen days.

'The frightening waves were like mountains,' he wrote. 'They would lift the ship up into the blue sky and then drop it as if down an abyss. They billowed and crashed, the noise splitting heaven from earth. We might all be drowned and left to rot at any moment.' The ship was badly damaged and after the storm abated could only drift helplessly at the mercy of the wind, waves – and the Japanese pirates who frequented the waters between the Yellow Sea and the South China Sea. Twice it was boarded by Chinese pirates who stripped it of its cargo, supplies and equipment.

To add insult to injury Choe and his companions were themselves mistaken for Japanese pirates and nearly killed when they finally washed up on the Chinese coast south of Shanghai. Choe Bu's knowledge of Chinese culture saved their lives and they began the long overland journey northwards and homewards through China. It took the party 135 days to reach Korea's northern border, including a twenty-five-day stay in Beijing when they were presented to Emperor Yingzong.

Throughout, Choe observed and noted the characteristics of local populations. As he progressed he contrasted the customs of the south with those of the north, writing with a philosophical compassion. For example, 'Women on the southern banks of the river were wearing black loose upper garments and pants. In terms of hair accessories, those in the south wear long and round accessories, while those in the north wear round and sharp ones.'

Back home, after the period of mourning for his father required by Korean custom, Choe presented his diary to King Seongjong, who was fascinated. Following the relocation of China's capital from southern Nanjing to Beijing in the north in 1421, no Korean delegation had visited the south for seventy years. Then and now, Choe's Bu's diary was a unique insight into the lives of people at all levels of fifteenth-century Chinese society.

LEFT: A line engraving of a fifteenth century merchant ship, much like the one Chloe would have travelled in.

Philip Henslowe, English theatre producer

(1550–1615)

The world of theatre owes much to the richness of English drama in the sixteenth and seventeenth centuries, in which playwrights Ben Johnson, Christopher Marlowe and William Shakespeare flourished. The diary of a contemporary theatrical entrepreneur is an invaluable companion to the period.

Philip Henslowe earned his money by various means, amassing considerable wealth as a landlord, dyer and starch-maker, money lender and dealer in goat skin. His wealth gave him status in high society, and he held appointments in the royal households of Elizabeth I of England and James VI and I – the first British monarch to reign over both England and Scotland.

He invested extensively in the theatrical arts and had shares in several theatres of the day including the Fortune, the Hope, and the Rose, as well as a number of acting companies, among them the Lord Strange's Men and the Lord Admiral's Men – which counted Henslowe's son-in-law Edward Alleyn among its leading actors. Henslowe and Alleyn worked closely together and Alleyn used his share of the profits to establish Dulwich College, where Henslowe's diary still resides and which would later be the alma mater of another giant of English literature, P. G. Wodehouse.

Henslowe's diary covers the period from 1592 to 1609, of which only 1599-1604 deal with theatre records. Philip Henslowe's entries are a mixture of receipts from performances of plays, expenses from the production of props, costumes and scenery, and notes on the hiring of actors and other business expenses. Although it is not a personal diary, it is a glimpse into an artistic world of global significance.

Henslowe rarely names the authors of his plays, as it was common practice at the time for aspiring playwrights to "borrow" the titles of successful dramas to promote their own works. Henslowe did have considerable success with Marlowe's *Doctor Faustus* and with plays titled *Hamlet, Henry VI: Part 1, Henry V, Taming of the Shrew* and *Titus Andronicus*, which most likely belonged to Shakespeare.

The English language was, in Henslowe's time, very much a spoken, not a written tongue. Henslowe himself used many different spellings of his own name, sometimes within the same document; and some of the diary entries take careful deciphering. One page lists the following:

> 'Item, ij marchepanes, & the sittie of Rome
> Item, viij viserdes; Tamberlyne brydell; j wooden matook
> Item; iij tymbrells, j dragon in fostes
> Item, j cauderm for the Jewe'

'Marchepane' is an older version of the word marzipan, but it's curious to find it connected to the city of Rome, which is presumably a backdrop for some scenes in Marlowe's *Doctor Faustus*. Visards were masks connected to *Tamburlaine*, another Marlowe play, in which the title character humiliates the King of Jerusalem by harnessing him with a bridle to Tamburlaine's chariot. Other items include a mattock which is a farm tool; a tumbrel which is a two-wheeled cart; and the cauldron which is a prop from Marlowe's play *The Jew of Malta* in which the unfortunate title character is boiled alive.

The 'dragon in Faustus' is something of a mystery: there is no dragon in *Doctor Faustus*, but perhaps there was once, and it was cut from the version we know today. Marlowe plays made up 12% of the 752 productions to which Henslowe refers, for – as he notes in his diary – 'there's money in Marlowe.'

ABOVE: An image of the Fortune Theatre in Barbican, London which was built by Philip Henslowe and William Alleyn in 1599-1600. The theatre cost £1,320 to build and opened in May 1601.

Matsudaira Ietada, Japanese Samurai

(1555–1600)

The diary of a samurai warrior from the Sengoku period of Japanese history – a time when rival factions were constantly at war – provides us with a specialised perspective of Japan becoming a unified nation.

Matsudaira Ietada kept his diary for seventeen years from 1575 to 1594. He was a *samurai*, an elite soldier sworn to unquestioning loyalty toward his *shōgun* patron. In Matsudaira's case, his patron was his older brother Tokugawa Ieyasu; and Matsudaira not only fought on his brother's behalf but raised one of his brother's children as his own.

Ieyasu is a central figure in Japanese history. He is regarded as one of the three "Great Unifiers", alongside Oda Nobunaga and Toyotomi Hideyoshi, thanks to whom the islands of Japan coalesced into a single national identity. Ietada's journal covers the years leading up to that unification. It records, for example, the occasion when, in 1583, Hideyoshi gave Ieyasu a falcon. Both men enjoyed the sport of falconry and the exchange of such birds was a diplomatic act much like China's policy of so-called "panda diplomacy" in the twenty-first century.

The unification of Japan was a slow and bloody process which required the defeat of powerful overlords, like the Takeda clan who were reluctant to give up their power. Ietada fought with the united armies of Ieyasu and Nobunaga against the Takeda clan at the Battle of Mikatagahara in 1575, which was a disastrous defeat for the allied forces. Revenge came three years later at the Battle of Nagashino. This was an overwhelming victory for the allies, beating superior Takeda manpower thanks to their use of firearms against the enemy's cavalry charges. The battle fatally weakened the Takeda clan and Nagashino is seen as the turning point in the Great Unifiers' campaign.

Ietada's diary also records his meetings with other soldiers. His description of the legendary black samurai Yasuke is our only source for the physical appearance of the man: 'Oda Nobunaga gave a stipend to a black man presented originally to him by the [Jesuit] missionaries. His body was wholly black, and he stood at six shaku and two sun (1.82m); name of Yasuke'. Nobunaga, like most other Japanese, had never seen a Black man, and at their first meeting ordered Yasuke to be scrubbed clean of his supposed body paint.

Meanwhile, following the collapse of the Takeda clan, others saw their own opportunities in the resulting power vacuum. Ishida Mitsunari, a former ally of Ietada's brother Ieyasu, challenged the alliance's authority, first in the government and from 1599 in the field.

When Mitsunari began to advance on Kyoto Ieyasu's castle at Fushimi stood in his way, and in 1599 Ieyasu gave command of the outpost to his brother Ietada. It was an order as hard to give as to obey. Fushimi could not be defended against Mitsunari's advancing hoard, and Ietada's first act was to send away some of the best warriors under his command, knowing that they would be better put to use elsewhere. He and his remaining troops fought to the death at the Battle of Fushimi Castle in August 1600, buying valuable time for the alliance, which prevailed decisively at the Battle of Sekigahara in October that year. Mitsunari was beheaded, and the Three Unifiers restored Japan to central government in 1603.

LEFT: A woodcut depiction of Matsudaira Ietada. Ietada took part in Nagashino and several subsequent battles and sieges which further advanced the cause. He was rewarded in 1590 with the first of a series of regional commands.

Lady Anne Clifford, disinherited English noble

(1590–1676)

Lady Anne Clifford's father died when she was fifteen and though she expected, as his eldest child, to inherit his estates and titles, her male relatives had other plans leading Anne to be deprived of her rightful inheritance for the next forty-five years.

Anne's father, George Clifford, owned estates throughout northwestern England, in the counties of Westmoreland, Cumberland and Yorkshire. By law Anne should have inherited them all, but George left them instead to his brother Francis, the oldest male heir. Anne rejected the £15,000 which was left to her in the will and spent the next forty years fighting to regain her proper due.

Despite opposition from her two husbands (both of whom she outlived) and words of discouragement from King James I of England, Anne persisted, encouraged by James' wife Queen Anne of Denmark. Lady Anne finally won her property back in 1643, at the age of fifty-three, when Francis Clifford's son died without heirs.

Anne's first husband was Richard Sackville, 3rd Earl of Dorset. Theirs was by some accounts a loving marriage, although the pair also had tempestuous arguments. When Anne turned down an offer of a further £14,000 to give up the pursuit of her property, Richard accepted it on her behalf and used this to settle his gambling debts. On another occasion, when he had won handsomely at cockfighting and entertained his friends lavishly with his winnings, Anne observed to him 'how good he was to everybody else and how unkind to me.'

Anne detested Richard's brother Edward, whom she suspected of scheming against her. When false rumour reached her that Edward had died in a duel in 1613, Anne was privately thrilled. Yet, the pair had some agreeable moments. In 1617 Anne wrote, 'I went abroad with my brother Sackville, sometimes early in the morning and sometimes after supper, he and I being kind and having better correspondence than we have had.'

When news reached Anne on July 24th 1652 that Edward had in reality passed away, her diary entry is devoid of any of the expected piety reserved for death. 'The 17th of this July being Saturday, died Edwd Sackville Earl of Dorset in great Dorset House in London,' she wrote, 'and he was buried within a while after in the Vault Wethiam Church in Sussex [beside] his wife and his eldest Brother my first Lord and many of their Ancestors of whose death Mr Christr Marsh brought me word to Skipton Castle the 24th Day of that Month.'

In later entries however she was less restrained. 'Mr Edward Earl of Dorset was the most bitter and earnest Enemy to me that ever I had,' she recalled towards the end of her life, 'but God Almighty delivered me most miraculously from all his crafty devices.' Anne added two Biblical references. 'Gen. C. 23 V. 5 for without the merciful power of that God it had been impossible for me to have stayed therein. Ps. 18 Ve 4, 43, 47, 48.'

The Psalms verses are particularly triumphant: 'The cords of death entangled me; the torrents of destruction overwhelmed me. ... He is the God who avenges me, who subdues nations under me, who saves me from my enemies. You exalted me above my foes; from a violent man you rescued me.'

RIGHT: A portrait of Lady Anne Clifford by English painter William Larkin, dated 1618.

ABOVE: *Isaac Ambrose, depicted here in a contemporary portrait. Ambrose ventured towards Presbyterianism, which emphasized strict spiritual discipline in daily life and a personal experience of Christian salvation.*

Isaac Ambrose, English Puritan

(1604–1664)

Ambrose was a seventeenth-century minister of religion who urged all Christians to keep a diary of their communion with God. His own daily entries describe in simple terms, his daily meditations in the secluded stillness of a northern English woodland.

The civil war in seventeenth-century England was as much a spiritual struggle as one for political power. Republicans sought the removal of a despotic king as head of state in favour of a democratic form of government; and this same desire for greater access to power drove a change in religious practice. Many wondered why if the ruling classes could exercise government without the interference of the king, could Christians not have direct prayer with God, without the intermediation of priests and bishops.

The official Church of England was established after Henry VIII's schism with Rome, and adopted many of the trappings of Roman Catholicism. The institution had become bloated with ceremony and often acted as a gatekeeper between God and the ordinary people. A movement grew of those no longer willing to conform to the Church of England's model of Christianity and one of the earliest forms of this non-conformity was Puritanism, an extreme form of Presbyterianism.

Isaac Ambrose began life as the son of a Church of England vicar and followed in his father's footsteps, taking up a succession of posts in the north of England culminating in an appointment as the vicar of the town of Preston in Lancashire under the patronage of Lady Margaret Hoghton. His living thus secured, it was in Lancashire that Isaac began to question the trappings of his religion. He took to going for long walks in the ancient woods of the Hoghton family estate, where an old stone tower provided a safe, quiet place in which to meditate.

Isaac recorded his insights in a diary, the use of which he described in a book some years later. 'We read,' he wrote, 'of many Ancients that were accustomed to keep Diaries or Day-books of their actions, and out of them to take an Account of their Lives: Such a Register (of God's Dealings towards him, and of his Dealings toward God in main Things) the Lord put into a poor Creature's Heart to keep in the Year 1641, ever since which Time he hath continued it, and once a Year purposes (by God's Grace) to examine himself by it.' He continued with some examples from his own diary of 1651.

'14 May

In a pleasant Wood, and sweet Walks in it, the Lord moved and enabled me to begin the Exercise of secret Duties: and after the prolegomena, or Duties in general, I fell on that Duty of watchfulness: The Lord then gave me to observe my former Negligence, and to make some Resolutions. I found the Lord sweet to me in the Conclusion of the Duty. Allelujah.'

'15 May

I fell on the duty of Self-trial, and in the Morning confessed my Sins before and since Conversion, wherein the Lord sweetly melted my Heart. In the Evening I perused my Diary for the last Year, wherein are many Passages of Mercies from God, and Troubles for sin, etc.'

Ambrose drifted further and further from the Church of England towards Presbyterianism. He quit his position at Preston in 1654; and in 1662, following the restoration of the monarchy, he and 2000 other ministers in a similar crisis of conformity were formally ejected from the established Church.

Peter Julius Coyet, Swedish envoy to England

(1618–1667)

Great Britain's diplomatic relations with its neighbours were understandably affected by the beheading of King Charles I in 1949. The succeeding ruler Lord Protector Oliver Cromwell, sought to make new agreements with many of them, including Sweden, with whom Britain found a common cause, recorded in the pages of their envoy's diary.

In Europe for much of the second millennium wars were begun, or at least justified, by religious differences. England in the sixteenth and seventeenth centuries seemed to change its official religion as often as it changed monarchs; and under Cromwell the nation was distinctly Presbyterian in nature.

Sweden, a monarchy under King Karl X, had some reservations about dealing with a country which beheaded its own monarch. Yet Sweden was also Presbyterian in the majority; and England was fighting a war against Catholic France. As the saying goes, 'my enemy's enemy is my friend'; and two skilled diplomats – ambassador Christer Bonde and envoy Peter Julius Coyet – travelled to London to negotiate agreements on such matters as the use of Swedish ports by British ships and the mutual interests of Swedish and British settlers along the Delaware river in the New World of North America.

The journals of both men offer interesting perspectives on a unique period of British history. Coyet's time in the capital was short – only eighteen months during 1655 and 1656 – and he was afterwards posted to the Netherlands where he negotiated two important European agreements: the Treaty of Roskilde between Sweden and its enemy Denmark, and the Treaty of Breda between England and its enemy the Netherlands.

In 1655 Coyet's job was to find common ground with the Presbyterian English and he found it in an outbreak of religious persecution by French Savoie of a Protestant sect known as the Waldensians or the Vaudois.

The Vaudois' attachment to an extremely ascetic version of Christianity, closer to English Puritanism than to Roman Catholicism, put it firmly at odds with France. The Duke of Savoy had ordered the Vaudois, 'in the hardest season of the winter, to quit their habitation upon penalty of loss of life and confiscation of their estates, unless they should within twenty days after the publication of the said edict make it appear that they had embraced the Roman Religion.' Terrible massacres of the Vaudois followed, and their suffering struck a chord with the newly liberated English Presbyterians.

Peter Coyet was impressed by this English compassion, and wrote in his diary on 25th May 1655: 'The persecution of the [Waldensians] by Savoy has much moved the Protector, who has contributed £2000 for their relief from his own means, and intends shortly to impose a tax [in fact a public appeal] through the entire kingdom for that purpose; and to write to the Duke of Savoy urging him to milder measures, and to making a safer place of refuge for them within his country.'

Cromwell did send envoys to Savoie, and at home he declared June 14th 1655 a day of fasting and self-denial in solidarity with the victims of French Catholicism, during which a collection would be taken. This was an enormous success, stirring up anti-Catholic sentiment and raising the sum of £38,097 7s. 3d., the largest donation in the country's history at the time. When a similar collection was held for the victims of the Great Fire of London ten years later, it only raised £16,201 9s. 9½d. in comparison.

RIGHT: Peter Julius Coyet acted as a Swedish envoy to England, Scotland and Ireland as ruled by Oliver Cromwell, pictured here taking the oath in 1653 to become Lord Protector.

ABOVE: An 1816 copperplate engraving of Mary Rich from Samuel Woodburn's Gallery of Rare Portraits Consisting of Original Plates.

Mary Rich, Countess of Warwick, Irish maid of honour

(1625–1678)

Mary Rich's diary extends to thousands of pages. She wrote almost every day during the final twelve years of her life and her words are a portal to the world of the Irish Protestant aristocracy, both in Ireland and in England.

Mary Rich was born Mary Boyle, the daughter of Lord Richard Boyle of Cork, in the port of Youghal on Ireland's south coast. Youghal is best known today as the place where Cromwell's Protestant troops landed in 1649 and began their violent efforts to subdue a Catholic rebellion in Ireland. Cromwell sought to exercise English authority over Ireland, as Queen Elizabeth had done before him, by confiscating lands and giving them to an immigrant English ruling class, which became known as the Protestant Ascendancy. Richard Boyle went to Ireland under Elizabeth's rule and was such an effective defender of the English cause in Ireland that Cromwell said of him, 'If there had been an Earl of Cork in every province, it would have been impossible for the Irish to have raised a rebellion'.

Sir Richard was, then, a considerable force of nature and his daughter, Mary was cast from the same mould. Characterised as stubborn and independent, she was known even to her loving father as 'my unruly daughter'. Mary refused bluntly to accept the marriage which had been arranged for her – to another member of the Ascendancy – and instead was married in secret to Charles Rich, the relatively poor younger son of the Earl of Warwick, who had nursed her through the measles.

It was a marriage born of love rather than convenience; but it proved an unhappy one. Charles was intemperate and a lifelong sufferer of gout, the pain of which made him most irritable. His bitterness was increased by the early deaths of their two children, and Mary frequently recorded arguments in her diary: 'My lord did so provoke me that I was surprised into a sudden disputing with him'; 'After I returned home, I fell into a foolish dispute with my lord'; 'I fell into a dispute with him wherein I was very passionately affected'; and so on.

Mary Rich also wrote an autobiography, a mere forty pages in length. It differs from her diary in many respects, withholding details of discord and unhappiness and painting a far more noble, and heroic depiction of her husband. The autobiography was clearly meant to be read by others; whereas the diary can be seen as a more candid account of her life – private and confessional.

Charles unexpectedly inherited the Earldom of Warwick in 1659 and thereafter the couple lived on his family estate in Essex. Mary began to keep her diary in 1666, and among its many narrative threads is the solace she found in religion. She was devoutly puritanical and tried as much as she could to live by a strong ethical code. Even when Mary's patience with her husband was tested, she was able to acknowledge at the end of the day, 'O, we do all offend! There's not a day of wedded life, if we count at its close the little, bitter sum of thoughts and words and looks unkind and froward, silence that chides, and woundings of the eye, but prostrate at each other's feet we should each night forgiveness ask'.

When Charles died in 1673, Mary was crippled with grief. 'This greatest trial of my life did for a long time disorder my frail house of clay,' she reflected, 'and made me have thoughts that my dissolution was near; which thoughts were not at all terrible or affrighting to me, but very pleasant and delightful.' For his part, Charles left to Mary all his estates and property, an unusual act at that time. Mary outlived him by five years.

Samuel Pepys, English civil servant

(1633–1703)

Samuel Pepys' diary owes its fame as much to the character of the man who wrote it as to the interesting times in which he lived. Pepys lived through the Great Plague in 1665 and the Great Fire of London of 1666, and recorded it all with wit, perspective and humanity.

Pepys began his celebrated diary, as so many of us do, on New Year's Day, in his case of 1660. He wrote for himself, not for an audience; and besides the eye-witness reports of history there are candid moments of confession and self-blame for his misdemeanours. Pepys wrote it in a form of shorthand code so that no one else might read the sometimes-shameful events of his days. The diary ends in 1669, the year his wife died, when he had lived only half of his lifespan.

Samuel Pepys was directly involved in the affairs of the country. He made his way successfully upwards through the English Civil Service through a combination of adroit political skills, considerable personal talent and a willingness to take the bribes which were frequently offered to him. He played a significant part in the transformation of the British Navy: from a haphazard affair to a more professional fighting force. In the process Pepys became, from humble beginnings, a very wealthy man.

He was one of the first people that King Charles II met after his restoration to the English throne in 1660, following the death of Oliver Cromwell. In that year Pepys was assigned unwittingly to the admiral whose ship sailed to Holland to bring the king back home from exile; and he maintained a close professional relationship with Charles thereafter, which can only have helped his career.

Under Charles II many of the pleasures of life which had been frowned upon and banned under Cromwell's Puritan regime were permitted once more. Samuel Pepys had no hesitation in indulging himself in these new guilty pleasures. He drank to excess and frequently had "dalliances" outside his marriage, often with his own maidservants. Samuel was particularly excited by visits to the theatre where, for the first time in history, women were now being allowed to perform. One of the first actresses of this new era was Nell Gwyn, with whom Pepys conducted an irregular but intimate relationship. Of an encounter with a 'Mrs Lane' in 1660, he wrote, 'I was exceedingly free in dallying with her, and she not unfree to take it'.

Pepys' eye-witness descriptions of the Great Fire of London, which raged for three days in 1666 and burnt his own house down, are compassionate and lyrical. He vividly observes the combustion of 'the houses, too, so very thick thereabouts, and full of matter of burning, as pitch and tarr, in Thames-street; and warehouses of oyle, and wines, and brandy, and other things,' the dangers of being 'almost burned with a shower of fire-drops' and the sound of 'the cracking of houses at their ruine.' He rowed out into the middle of the River Thames to get a closer look, and saw 'everybody endeavouring to remove their goods, and flinging into the river or bringing them into lighters that lay off; poor people staying in their houses as long as till the very fire touched them.'

ABOVE: *An oil painting of Samuel Pepys by John Hayls, completed in 1666 and referenced in Pepys' diary.*
RIGHT: *An excerpt from Samuel Pepys' diary, showcasing his handwriting.*
LEFT: *A woodcut depiction of the Great Fire of London, dated to around 1883.*

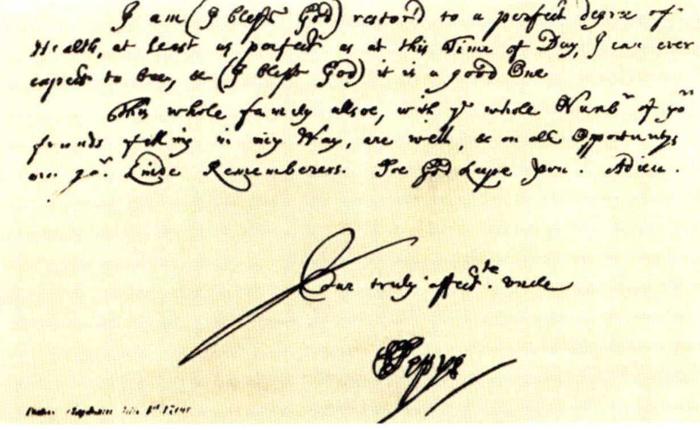

I am (I bless God) restor'd to a perfect degree of Health, at least as perfect as at this Time of Day I can ever expect to have, and (I bless God) it is a good One.
This whole family also, with the whole Numb^r of yor friends falling in my Way, are well, and on all Opportunitys are yor Kinde Rememberers. Soe God keepe you. Adieu.

Your truly affect^te Uncle
S Pepys

ABOVE: A contemporary depiction of the alleged atrocities committed during the 1641 Irish Rebellion.

Tarlach Ó Mealláin, Irish Franciscan friar

(1641–1650)

Britain's attempts to colonise Ireland were supported by waves of "plantations" – the forced implanting of predominantly Protestant English and Scottish overlords among the native Roman Catholic population of the island. One Irish monk was given the job of documenting the ensuing bloody rebellion.

Three English monarchs tried to take over Ireland by the method of plantations – Mary I, Elizabeth I and James I (twice), between 1556 and 1620. The assumption by the incoming settlers – mostly Scottish in the north and English in the south – that they had a God-given superiority over the Irish, was naturally met with resentment.

As the implanted population grew, Irish resentment was fuelled by discrimination against the Irish and their religion, until it erupted into full-blown rebellion in 1641. Known sometimes as the Irish Confederate Wars and sometimes as the Eleven Years' War, the rebellion was part of the Three Kingdoms War, in which Charles I of England was fighting uprisings in both Ireland and Scotland.

In Ireland, the rebellion was led by the O'Neill clan who wanted to see a reduction in plantations and an increase in self-government. It was the most violent conflict in Irish history, a harrowing process of ethnic cleansing, atrocities and starvation from scorched earth tactics on both sides. From 1641 until the war ended in 1653, there may have been as many as 600,000 deaths from famine, disease and fighting.

Felim O'Neill was the leader of the rebel alliance. When a community of Franciscan monks had been expelled from Armagh after a sixteenth-century plantation, an ancestor of O'Neill had offered them land and protection on the shores of a lake which is now called Friary Loch. In 1641 one of the friars, Tarlach Ó Mealláin, was Felim O'Neill's personal chaplain, and O'Neill instructed him to keep a record of the conflict to come. Tarlach accompanied O'Neill at many of the rebellion engagements and was an eyewitness to the horrors of the war. The Franciscan monk recorded it all in hastily kept notes in a journal, with a view to writing them up later into a full history of the uprising.

Terrible deeds were enacted in the name of religion and worse were alleged, by both sides. Much of the loss of life was caused by scorched earth – the practice of destroying crops and livestock to deprive one's enemies of food. Tarlach described the measures put into place to stop the theft of food, and the appalling lengths which people went to, to feed themselves:

'It was also resolved that whoever should steal a cow or horse, steed or gelding, sheep or goat or the value of any of these, would have a like amount confiscated from him, if he were a man of means; or hanged, if he were a man of no means. ... There are people in the country, Ó Catháins, O'Devlins, O'Haras, and the people of Iveagh, all of Clandeboy and the Route [reduced to] eating horses and steeds; stealing; carrying off cats; dogs; eating corpses; rotten leather; and undressed leather.'

The war ended in defeat for the rebels and led, 260 years later, to the unhappy partitioning of Ireland which still exists in the twenty-first century. Tarlach Ó Mealláin's diary remains a touchstone for those who wish to see the reunification of the island.

Daniel Defoe, English author and spy

(1660-1731)

Daniel Defoe was far too young to remember the arrival of the Great Plague in London in 1665. Yet his *Journal of the Plague Year* is praised for its veracity and accuracy of detail. Defoe didn't write it, but he knew a man who did.

Daniel Defoe was only five years old when the Great Plague struck London. In adult life he was not only the author of celebrated novels *Robinson Crusoe* and *Moll Flanders* but a political campaigner and sometime spy for the English king William III. Accustomed to deception in the latter role, it was at least legitimate for him to dissemble in his fictional works – he passed off *Robinson Crusoe* as the autobiographical work of the titular hero, and *Moll Flanders* as being 'written from her own memorandums'.

Even Daniel Defoe is not his real name. He was born plain Daniel Foe yet adopted the De to give his name more impact. He is known to have used at least 198 pen names; and *A Journal of the Plague Year* is credited to 'a citizen who continued all the while in London' and attributed to a certain HF. HF is widely believed to be Henry Foe, Daniel's uncle, who did indeed live in London throughout 1665.

A Journal of the Plague Year is based on Uncle Henry's own journals, with considerable additional research by Defoe. Defoe was meticulous in his attention to detail, and his descriptions of Africa in another novel, *Captain Singleton*, must surely have been acquired from someone with first-hand knowledge of the continent.

Combining his research with his uncle's recollections, the Journal makes compelling and harrowing reading. The population of London increased sharply after the restoration of the monarchy, and overcrowding was a factor in the spread of the disease, compounded by 'a strong belief,' Defoe wrote, 'that the plague would not come to the city, nor into Southwark, nor into Wapping or Ratcliff at all. ... Many removed from the suburbs ... into those eastern and south sides as for safety, and, as I verily believe, carried the plague amongst them there'.

Defoe quotes the records of weekly mortality which were recorded at the time. 'Now there died four within the city, one in Wood Street, one in Fenchurch Street and two in Crooked Lane.' The numbers climbed, and at its height 8000 died in a single week, 3000 in a single day. He describes the symptoms – 'those spots they called the tokens were really gangrenous spots, or mortified flesh in small knobs as broad as a little silver penny, and as hard as a piece of callous or horn ... no instrument could cut them, so that many died roaring mad with the torment'.

'Dead carts', preceded by a warning bell, brought piles of corpses to the mass burial pits, although in some areas the alleys were too narrow and hand carts from the markets were put to use. Defoe recalls the agony of one cartman 'oppressed with a dreadful weight of grief indeed, having his wife and several children all in the cart. ... No sooner was the cart turned round and the bodies shot into the pit promiscuously ... but he cried out aloud.' A quarter of London's population died in 1665.

Defoe brings all his story-telling talent to *A Journal of the Plague Year*, leading many to consider it a work of fiction. But the authenticity of his voice has the dreadful ring of truth about it.

RIGHT: A seventeenth century portrait of Daniel Defoe, author of Treasure Island*.*

ABOVE: An oil painting of American lawyer and writer William Byrd II, from around 1700.

William Byrd II, Colonial American diarist

(1674–1744)

We might never have heard of William Byrd, a Virginian plantation owner, had his very private diary not been discovered in the 1940s. Written in shorthand to keep its secrets from prying eyes, the account reveals a man whose lust for life was so often accompanied by the hope that God would forgive him.

'Bless God for granting me so many years,' wrote William Byrd on his thirty-sixth birthday. 'I wish I had spent them better.' He was not a good man, certainly not by modern standards. He beat enslaved people regularly for trivial offences, for which he showed no remorse; and was promiscuously unfaithful to his wife, for which he asked God, but not her, for forgiveness.

Byrd's diary records the events of his days in a consistent, matter-of-fact tone, taking the good with the bad and the sinful with the homely. One record from May 6th 1709 explains how 'In the afternoon Colonel Ludwell returned and brought us the bad news that Captain Morgan had lost his ship in Margate Roads by a storm as likewise had several others. My loss was very great in this ship where I had seven hogs-heads of skins and 60 hogsheads of heavy tobacco. The Lord gives and the Lord has taken away – blessed be the name of the Lord. In the evening Mr. Clayton and Mr. Robinson came and confirmed the same bad news. However I ate a good supper of mutton and asparagus. Then we went to dance away sorrow.'

And on October 6th the same year, 'I rose at 6 o'clock and said my prayers and ate milk for breakfast. Then I proceeded to Williamsburg, where I found all well. I went to the capitol where I sent for the wench to clean my room and when I came I kissed her and felt her, for which God forgive me. The I went to see the President, whom I found indisposed in his ears. I dined with [name omitted] on beef. About 10 o'clock I went to my lodgings. I had good health but wicked thoughts, God forgive me.'

His treatment of his enslaved people was terrible. Two, used as house servants, came in for frequent punishment. 'Jenny and Eugene were whipped,' he notes on February 8th 1709 without mentioning the reason. Eugene eventually absconded, but on June 10th, 'George brought home my boy Eugene. Eugene was whipped for running away and had the [bit] put on him.' On September 3rd, 'In the afternoon I beat Jenny for throwing water on the couch.' On December 1st, 'Eugene was whipped again for pissing in bed and Jenny for concealing it.' And on December 3rd, 'Eugene pissed abed again for which I made him drink a pint of piss.'

At the end of every day's entry, Byrd took a moment to assess his own mental and physical condition, usually recorded with the phrase 'I had good health, good thoughts, and good humor, thanks be to God.' Byrd's lust was unbridled. He imposed himself on his servants and enslaved people, had affairs with other men's wives, including his own wife's sister – and occasionally on his wife herself, all of which he recorded in his diary. 'In the afternoon my wife and I had a little quarrel which I reconciled with a flourish. It is to be observed that the flourish was on the billiard table.'

Mary Cowper, English courtier

(1685–1724)

If you can't tell your diary what you really think about your colleagues, who can you tell? Mary Cowper had friends in very high places, and a dry wit with which to characterise them – either in the privacy of her journals or directly to their faces.

Mary Cowper was Lady of the Bedchamber to Caroline, Princess of Wales, wife of the future George II. Her husband William Cowper was Britain's first Lord High Chancellor. Something of a power couple at the court of George I, they both played important parts in their nation's history. William was a close confidant of both Queen Anne and George I, and Mary played an important role in settling a right royal domestic dispute.

George I resented his son's greater popularity with the public. When the younger George insulted his father's friend the Duke of Newcastle in 1717, the king angrily confined his son and his daughter-in-law Caroline to their quarters, denying them access to the palace and to their children. Mary acted as an intermediary for Caroline, who was eventually allowed her freedom from what had effectively been house arrest.

The rift between father and son was never fully healed. The king suspected his confidant William Cowper of taking his son's side and Cowper resigned in 1718. Mary's diaries regularly refer to events and people of political and social importance. They cover the period from 1714 to 1720 – but the years from 1717 to 1718 are missing. Mary burned them, and it is assumed that she did so because they contained compromising information about her husband's position in the quarrel, or of intemperate words from Caroline about the king.

There was often rivalry among the women of the royal court to secure the attention of the King for their husbands, which in turn would raise their own status. Mary was a shrewd, if occasionally catty observer of such jostling for position. Isabel Danvers was, like Mary, a Lady of the Bedchamber; and of Isabel's marriage to the Bishop of Derry, she commented, 'She married an Irish bishop who hoped to be made an English Bishop by marrying one of the Queen's dressers, but, I don't know how it happened, he missed his aim, and got only one of the frightfullest, disagreeablest wives in the Kingdom.'

A friend of Mary's, Sarah Churchill, Duchess of Marlborough, described Isabel as 'not looking human'. Despite their friendship, Mary observed of Sarah that she 'loved power even more than the Duke [her husband] did.'

Many other women became the target for her tongue, as Mary's report of February 13th 1716 reveals: 'I was to dine at Baron Bernstorff's but excus'd myself because I was ill. The Ladys that were there came here in the afternoon, Mademoiselle Schutz a very unreasonable body, would take no hints that I wish'd to be alone but took a pleasure in staying because I was uneasie at it.'

And the following day, 'I have had a letter from Mademoiselle Schutz to offer to come & stay with me all day. I thank her for nothing. I had too much of her impertinence last night. I answered her with writing to her that I should be glad to see her any other time, but now my Lord was so ill I had resolved to shut myself up with him, & that I was sure that no body that was really my friend, would take it ill of me that I gave all my time to a husband to whom I ow'd so much, & who stood so much in need of my assistance.'

ABOVE: A portrait of Mary Cowper by her contemporary Sir Godfrey Kneller, a German-born painter.

St Francis preaching to the birds
Gilbert White
1720
1793
1920

Gilbert White, English naturalist and Anglican cleric

(1720–1793)

Every day from 1758 until his death, Gilbert White kept a diary. He did not record world events; he did not keep up with local gossip; he did not catalogue any profound personal journey. Gilbert marked the endless cycle of life, death and rebirth of nature in one small English country village.

Gilbert White was born in Selborne, a village in Hampshire in which his grandfather (also Gilbert White) was the vicar. He studied at Oriel College, Oxford and was ordained in 1749. His professional life thereafter consisted of a series of curacies in Hampshire and the neighbouring Wiltshire, including four separate spells back in Selborne. Gilbert returned permanently to Selborne in 1758 following the death of his father, and lived in the house into which he had been born for the rest of his life.

His was a small life, unadventurous, undemanding. Gilbert tended to the needs of a small flock of parishioners, and even today the parish of Selborne has fewer than 1500 inhabitants. Gilbert studied nature, both in his garden and further afield in the countryside around Selborne. Over thirty-five years he observed and recorded the life cycles of his local flora and fauna through the changing of the seasons. In so doing Gilbert White changed almost single-handedly the study of natural history, which had previously relied largely on the dissection of dead specimens. The pioneering naturalist Charles Darwin acknowledged in 1870 his debt to Gilbert White who, a century earlier conducted a rich correspondence with other zoologists. His diary and those letters make up White's best-known book, *The Natural History of Selborne*, which was published by his brother Benjamin White four years before Gilbert's death and has not been out of print since.

White observed all forms of life. On May 20th 1777 he meditated on the fact that 'earthworms, though in appearance a small and despicable link in the chain of nature, yet, if lost, would make a lamentable chasm. For, to say nothing of half the birds, and some quadrupeds, which are almost entirely supported by them, worms seem to be the great promoters of vegetation, which would proceed but lamely without them.' For this recognition of nature as an interconnected cycle, White is regarded as the first ecologist.

His great interest was bird life and in particular the seasonal visits of swallows and swifts – White was fascinated by their migration patterns. By tuning into birdsong, he was able to distinguish, for the first time the three species – chiffchaff, willow warbler and wood warbler – which had previously been classed together as willow wrens. Gibert's pleasure in nature exudes from his descriptive daily entries, as he shown when writing about owls:

'About an hour before sunset (for then the mice begin to run) they sally forth in quest of prey, and hunt all round the hedges of meadows and small enclosures for them, which seem to be their only food. In this irregular country we can stand on an eminence and see them beat the fields over like a setting-dog, and often drop down in the grass or corn. I have minuted these birds with my watch for an hour together, and have found that they return to their nests, the one of them or the other, about once in five minutes.'

LEFT: These stained glass windows at St Mary's Church, Selborne commemorate Gilbert White's life. They were fitted in 1920, showing St Francis and the Birds, including birds referenced in White's book The Natural History of Selborne.

Jacob Elet, Dutch eighteenth century factor on the Slave Coast

(recorded 1721-1740)

Western Africa was in a state of political upheaval in the early eighteenth century. The Atlantic Slave Trade was paid for with European goods, creating wealth of a kind for Africans in positions of power. A little-known diary opens a small window onto one expanding African kingdom.

The kingdom of Dahomey, in southern modern-day Benin, has existed since around 1600. Today it has no constitutional role in Benin but survives as an apolitical and economic influence in the country. At the start of the eighteenth century however it was expanding rapidly under the rule of three kings – Houegbadja (who first unified the kingdom) and his sons Akaba and Agaja.

Agaja developed a standing Dahomese army of around 10,000 men, women and children which was well-disciplined, well-equipped and well-paid. With it he seized the kingdoms of Allada and Whydah, both major players in the slave trade, and sold his captured enemies to dealers from the European empires of France, Portugal, England and the Netherlands. Historians still debate Agaja's subsequent role in the trade: whether he continued to conduct it in order to phase it out, to enrich his kingdom or to enrich himself. He needed gunpowder for his weapons, cowrie shells for his soldiers' wages and fine European cloth for his wives, all of which were supplied by the Atlantic trade.

Agaja was a shrewd negotiator, and had good working relationships with Britain, Portugal and France. He disliked the Dutch however and in 1732 he kidnapped three employees of the Dutch West India Company after an attack on the fort at Jakin on the Benin coast, and held them hostage to his interests in slavery which had been thwarted at Jakin.

Enter Jacob Elet, chief factor for the company's fort at Accra, west of Dahomey. Elet had been posted to the region in 1721 and was well versed in the slave trade; in one diary entry he writes of 'young slaves, which cannot be bought nowadays for [such a] price.' He was charged with going to Agaja to negotiate the release of his colleagues. Jakin was a Portuguese outpost, and Elet took with him its commander Antonio de Pinto Carneiro in the hope that Portugal's better relationship with Agaja would ease negotiations. Four other Europeans travelled with them, and a train of eighty-four African porters to carry the comforts and essentials of life on the road. Jacob kept a journal of the trip, and everything we know about him comes from those daily entries.

Jacob Elet's journal illustrates the prevailing attitude of Europeans, that people with different coloured skin must necessarily be inferior to the White man. Although he makes a distinction between Africans of different locations – he refers to 'Appase neegers' and 'Dahommese neegers', Appa negroes and Dahomese negroes – it is their skin colour that defines them. They are not 'negroes from Appa' or 'negroes from Dahomey.' And when he describes Agaja in the most respectful terms after their meeting, he nevertheless uses the word 'barbaar' – barbarian.

Elet successfully negotiated the release of the hostages in return for the promise of a share of the Atlantic Slave Trade through Jakin. Unfortunately, the Dutch West India Company preferred to trade through the port of Appa, which was not under Dahomey control. Agaja felt that Elet had deceived him, and in revenge he destroyed the Appa trading post. Elet, now probably unpopular with his compatriots on the slave coast, was framed for corruption, acquitted but sent back to Holland in 1740. No further record of his life survives after that; but he is immortalised by his diary.

ABOVE: The Dutch West India Company, for which Elet worked, operated for almost 170 years and had jurisdiction over areas affected by the Atlantic Slave trade in Africa, Brazil, The Caribbean and North America.

ABOVE: An eighteenth century depiction of a village in East Sussex, taken from a weekly newspaper.

Thomas Turner, English shopkeeper

(1729–1793)

In today's society we could all do with someone like Thomas Turner. The man for whom the term "pillar of the community" might have been coined did everything for his neighbours, and thankfully wrote it all down.

For a small village, East Hoathly in England's south-eastern corner has several famous sons. Pirate John Dann, who terrorised the Indian Ocean in the seventeenth and eighteenth centuries, was born there in 1660; it was the birthplace in 1950 of Tony Banks, keyboard player and founding member of rock group Genesis; and it is where Thomas Turner ran his shop.

Turner sold everything – stationery, haberdashery, clothes, tobacco, hardware, groceries, liquor and coffins. As Charles Dickens noted after reading extracts from Turner's diaries, 'in the parlour behind his shop he made entries not only as a tradesman of his dealings with his customers, but as a husband, vestryman, neighbour, and a man of his home life, and his dealings with society at large'. The entries, which he wrote over eleven years in 111 notebooks, are an invaluable historic record of the historic way of English village life.

Thomas kept his journal in handwritten script, recording financial dealings as well as the events of the day. He was comparatively well educated – an avid reader of Shakespeare and other authors – and in addition to his work as a shopkeeper he used his facility with words and numbers for the benefit of other villagers. Turner helped out with wills and other legal matters, arranged loans, and taught his skills to others. He served in various capacities with the village church, assisting the poor of the parish; he played in the village cricket team; and he travelled widely between London and the south coast of England to deal with suppliers, often stopping on the way home for an alcoholic refreshment.

The diary begins in 1754, a year after his marriage to Peggy Slater and just before the birth of their only child, about whom he was forced to write on January 16th 1755: 'This morning about 1 o'clock I had the misfortune to lose my little boy Peter, aged 21 weeks, 3 days.' Married life was tempestuous, for which his drinking must take some responsibility. Entries such as this one from February 10th 1756 are common: 'Oh, what have I here to say—the old story again repeated—more words again between me and my wife. Sure it is a most terrible and unhappy circumstance we cannot live agreeable together.' Yet like many such marriages, there was affection and tenderness underneath and when Peggy died in 1764 his loss was palpable.

Thomas clearly liked a drink and often berated himself for his intemperance, as on Sunday March 28th 1762 he wrote 'I came home about 6:50, though I cannot say thoroughly sober. Yet I think it almost impossible to be otherwise with the quantity of liquor I drank. But however so it was, and notwithstanding the many resolutions I have taken, and which I have hereto as often broken as made, I hope once more to assume so much fortitude and resolution as to conquer the weakness of my brains by an entire abstinence from any liquor, strong.'

The diary ends in 1765, much as it began, a few months after the wedding of Thomas Turner and Molly Hicks, his second wife. In his final entry Thomas wrote, 'I begin once more to be a little settled and am happy in my choice.' After so much introspection about his first wife, his final sentence is, 'Well, here let us drop the subject and begin a new one.'

Elizabeth Sandwith Drinker, American Quaker

(1735–1807)

It's hard to keep up a diary and many cover only a few years of their writers' lives. What a treasure trove Elizabeth Drinker's is, written almost daily for forty-nine years. The Pennsylvania Quaker witnessed great change in American history, and in herself from youth to grandmotherhood.

Elizabeth began keeping a diary when she was twenty-three, three years before she was courted and married to a young merchant called Henry Drinker. Both were Quakers, members of the anti-hierarchical Society of Friends who got their Quaker nickname after their founder George Fox told a judge to 'quake before the authority of God'. If Elizabeth's diary contained nothing else, it would be a rare record of an entire eighteenth-century marriage – as she died only two years before Henry.

The greatest historical event to occur during Elizabeth Drinker's life was the American War of Independence. As Quakers, Henry and Elizabeth were pacifists and tried to avoid any involvement. Henry, like many of his Quaker friends, was accused of treachery for not supporting the independent cause and was imprisoned for a year. Elizabeth met with both Martha and George Washington in unsuccessful attempts to have her husband released early. During Henry's absence she was obliged to billet a British army officer, whom, despite the inconvenience, they befriended and corresponded with after his departure and until his death later in the conflict.

Henry's prosperity gave Elizabeth the privilege and comfort to continue writing her diary throughout their time together. They had five children and much of the diary concerns her role as a housewife and mother. The children had frequently to be nursed through sickness or injury – all survived to adulthood – and Elizabeth herself suffered from constant poor health. In her diary, Elizabeth had frequent occasion to describe the primitive levels of medical care which were available at the time. She spent a lifetime taking pills of more or less questionable efficacy, and in the last decade of her life observed that 'a mixture of good with the bad, makes the pill of life go down'.

Dr Kuhn, who attended her regularly, was a great believer in blood-letting. On November 16th 1793 'he advised the loss of 10 ounces of blood, which was taken from my right arm before 12 o'clock, by John Hailer. My cough continues very hard.' The following morning, 'my husband weighed the Bowl with the blood yesterday, 22½ oz. He weighed ye [empty] bowl today, 9½ oz; so that instead of 10 ounces, I lost thirteen.'

Philadelphia where the Drinkers lived, suffered an outbreak of Yellow Fever that year, and Elizabeth's record of the suffering, including the sad decline and death of her friend Sally Dawson, reflects her sense of helplessness. 'Thus it is – a pretty girl, in the bloom of youth, with a high and independent spirit, is taken off the stage of life in no more than 5 days illness. A lesson for both the young and old.' Medical science did not yet understand the causes of the disease and was therefore powerless to treat it.

Elizabeth Drinker writes of many social conditions now rather improved – the role of women, and of African Americans, with whom Quakers found common cause as victims of persecution. In the first few months of her diary, on March 1st 1759, she highlights another discipline in which much progress has been made: 'Pulled out a tooth in the evening, which the tooth drawer had drawn before and replaced.'

RIGHT: A seventeenth century drawing of a Quaker woman, seen here in similar garb to that which Drinkwater may have donned.

ABOVE: A portrait of John Adams in Philadelphia by Gilbert Stuart.

John Adams, Second President of the United States

(1735–1826)

The diaries of many Presidents of the United States have been preserved for posterity. Adams' diaries, mostly in tiny notebooks just six inches by four (150x10cm), are fascinating because they cover the years before and after the United States of America won its independence from Britain.

Adams was a founding father of the United States of America. A committed supporter of republicanism, he worked with Thomas Jefferson on writing the Declaration of Independence, insisting that Jefferson be credited with it because: 'Reason first, you are a Virginian, and a Virginian ought to appear at the head of this business. Reason second, I am obnoxious, suspected, and unpopular. You are very much otherwise. Reason third, you can write ten times better than I can.'

He was, however, slow to support the cause. Although John Adams opposed the tariffs and taxes on American goods which sparked the rebellion, he was a lawyer by profession and believed that a just resolution through legal and political channels was preferable, while remaining under the jurisdiction of the British crown. It was the famous Boston Tea Party, when £10,000-worth of British tea was destroyed in 1773 in protest at the British East India Company's monopoly on the commodity, which finally persuaded Adams of the need for independence. He wrote in his diary that the protest was 'the Grandest Event' in the history of the movement and was an 'absolutely and indispensably' unavoidable result of British actions.

Three years earlier, the British had called on Adams' professional services. Boston was again the setting. On March 5th 1770, British troops opened fire on a large crowd which had gathered to hurl abuse and objects at them. Three people died instantly and ten were injured, of whom two died later of their wounds. Republicans seized on the incident as propaganda, dubbing it the Boston Massacre, while the British played it down as the Incident on King Street. Nine British soldiers and four members of the public were charged with murder; but lawyers whom the British authorities approached to defend them declined to do so, fearful perhaps of giving such a public display of support to the Crown.

John Adams, whose republicanism was already well known, accepted the brief, secure in his belief in a defendant's right to counsel and the principle of presumption of innocence. It was a principled, honourable and – amongst his friends – unpopular position to take. The ensuing trial was one of the first in US legal history to use a dying declaration, by of one of the victims of the massacre, as evidence. Two of the accused had undoubtedly deliberately shot into the mob, and were branded for their crimes. Adams however secured the acquittal of the remaining seven. He noted in his diary:

'The Part I took in Defence of Cptn. Preston and the Soldiers, procured me Anxiety, and Obloquy enough. It was, however, one of the most gallant, generous, manly and disinterested Actions of my whole Life, and one of the best Pieces of Service I ever rendered my Country. Judgment of Death against those Soldiers would have been as foul a Stain upon this Country as the Executions of the Quakers or Witches, anciently. As the Evidence was, the Verdict of the Jury was exactly right. This however is no Reason why the Town should not call the Action of that Night a Massacre, nor is it any Argument in favour of the Governor or Minister, who caused them to be sent here. But it is the strongest Proofs of the Danger of Standing Armies.'

Janet Schaw, Scottish traveller

(1737-1800)

It was the journey of a lifetime. Janet Schaw set sail in 1774 from Leith, the seaport of the city of Edinburgh, bound for North Carolina. She met colonial relatives, enslaved Africans, the rich and poor, and experienced at first-hand storms at sea and the prelude to American independence.

Janet Schaw was a distant cousin of the Scottish novelist Sir Walter Scott. Although we have no image of her, portraits exist of one of her brothers and of her mother, suggesting that she was from a prosperous family. Her social status and good education make the journal she kept during her voyage a lively, literate account. Janet was unafraid to express her opinions bluntly, sometimes humorously, and her attitudes are those of her time and nationality, particularly toward enslaved people, the poor and those in America impudent enough to seek independence from Great Britain.

Janet was travelling with her brother, Alexander, who was emigrating to America. Another brother, Robert, had already settled there, and they planned to visit him on his North Carolina ranch, Schawfield. The ship carried other passengers too, and an illicit cargo of emigrants smuggled aboard and dreadfully treated by the ruthless captain of the vessel. All became characters in the pages of Miss Schaw's diary.

Their journey took them around the north coast of Scotland, the most dangerous tides in Britain, and across the Atlantic where in storms they lost all the livestock and food overboard on which they depended to survive. After seven weeks they arrived in Antigua where they rested before continuing to the North American seaboard. Janet returned via Lisbon in Portugal, still recovering from the devastating earthquake of 1755.

Her journal was intended from the start to be read by others. Three hand-written copies of it survive, evidence that it was widely circulated among her family back in Scotland. The accounts are conversational, often addressing the intended readers directly; and it is vividly descriptive of the high dramas and unfamiliar sights of the journey.

Schaw has much to say on every subject. When she visits her brother, Robert, she is unimpressed with 'the American methods of cultivating his plantation. Had he followed the style of an East Lothian farmer, with the same attention and care, it would now have been an Estate worth double what it is. Mrs. Schaw was shocked at the mention of our manuring the ground, and declared she never would eat corn that grew thro' dirt. Indeed she is so rooted an American, that she detests everything that is European, yet she is a most excellent wife and a fond mother.'

Janet Schaw disapproved deeply of the rebellion brewing in America and abandoned her plans to remain there. In Wilmington she witnessed a ramshackle parade of new rebel volunteers, 'preceded by a very ill beat-drum and a fiddler, who was also in his shirt with a long sword and a cue at his hair, who played with all his might. They made indeed a most unmartial appearance.'

Janet recounted that she would have laughed out loud had not the servant of one of her friends been driven out of town and almost tarred and feathered for smiling at the sight. That evening she made one of the American officers, Colonel Howe, read a passage from Shakespeare in which Falstaff describes his ragtag men in similarly disparaging terms. Howe quietly closed the book and whispered, 'You will certainly get yourself tarred and feathered; shall I apply to be executioner? I am going to seal this up. Adieu.'

ABOVE: A satirica cartoon entitled A society of Patriotic Ladies, at Edenton, in North Carolina. *Schaw's story gives an insight into a woman's experience during the foundation of "the new America".*

ABOVE: A portrait of the Ladies of Llangollen at Audley End. Their letters and this lithograph are held by the National Library of Wales.

Eleanor Charlotte Butler, one of the "Ladies of Llangollen"

(1739–1829)

Two women living together in domestic bliss may not turn heads today, but in the eighteenth century Eleanor Butler and Sarah Ponsonby attracted attention from the highest in the land. Eleanor's diary reveals the truth about the quiet, well-ordered life of the two recluses.

Eleanor and Sarah met when Eleanor was twenty-nine and Sarah thirteen. Both were unhappy in their lives, under pressure to make unsuitable marriages, and quickly formed a tight bond with each other, based on their shared needs to escape the demands of their families in Ireland. In 1778, they ran away from their homes together, armed with pistols and disguised as men, intending to sail for England with the romantic idea of living together in an English country cottage.

Eleanor and Sarah's families recaptured them only two miles short of the port of Waterford and brought them back home, but their friendship persisted and, eventually they were allowed to leave again. They settled not in England but in North Wales, where they bought a modest cottage on the outskirts of Llangollen in 1780. The pair sent for Sarah Ponsonby's childhood maid Mary Caryll, who remained with them for the rest of her life. Mary died in 1809, Eleanor in 1829 and Sarah in 1831; and all three are buried together in Llangollen beneath the same gravestone.

The life of these women was a quiet one. Thursday 22nd September 1785 was, from Eleanor's diary, a fairly typical day:

'Up at Seven. Dark Morning, all the Mountains enveloped in mist. Thick Rain. A fire in the Library, delightfully comfortable, Breakfasted at half past Eight. From nine 'till one writing. My Beloved drawing Pembroke Castle – from one to three read to her – after dinner Went hastily around the gardens. Rain'd without interruption the entire day – from Four 'till Ten reading to my Sally – She drawing – from ten 'till Eleven Sat over the Fire Conversing with My beloved. A Silent, happy Day.'

Their greatest extravagance was their cottage Plas Newydd (meaning "New Home" in Welsh), which they transformed from a humble cottage to miniature Gothic palace, using oak timbers reclaimed from old buildings and furniture and adding much stained glass. There was local gossip about the nature of the ladies' friendship, although nothing in Eleanor Butler's diary suggests anything more than an affectionate platonic love between the two.

Their convent-like existence was intriguing; their house was striking; they wore short hair and dressed in what visitors thought to be gentlemanly attire, although Llangollen locals considered it only sensible clothing for the north Welsh climate. As word spread, people came to stare, then to speak to them, and finally to be invited in. Poets and novelists began to call – William Wordsworth wrote a poem about them – as well as the great minds of the day such as Josiah Wedgwood and Charles Darwin. The English aristocracy were amused by the pair, and Lady Lonsdale described Eleanor as 'very clever, very odd'.

One notable visitor was another famous diarist, Anne Lister of Yorkshire, who recorded her own lesbian affairs in a secret code. She was naturally curious about the living arrangements of the Ladies of Llangollen; but when she asked 'if they were classical' – an oblique reference to the Ancient Greek lesbian poet Sappho – Sarah replied only, 'No ... Thank God from Latin & Greek I am free.'

Georg Pausch, German soldier in British service

(1740–1795)

When Britain realised that it had an American revolution on its hands, it did not have the military manpower to deal with the rebellion alone. The government of the time bought in mercenaries from several European states to deal with the shortfall, including the Hesse-Hanau Artillery Company, in which Major Georg Pausch served.

It is estimated that as many as one in three of the soldiers whom Britain sent to fight in the American War of Independence were not British. Germany, not yet the unified country it is today, consisted of several states, of which one of the lesser examples was the short-lived kingdom of Hesse-Hanau. William VIII of neighbouring Hesse-Cassel created Hesse-Hanau for his grandson in 1760, but by 1821 it had been reabsorbed into Hesse-Cassel and, only sixty-one years after its founding, Hesse-Hanau disappeared altogether.

At the time of the American War, both states sent troops to support Britain. Little is known of Georg Pausch before or after his involvement in North America, but the detailed diary which he kept from the moment he left his Hesse-Hanau home until his capture by American rebels at the Battle of Saratoga is a primary source for students of the conflict.

The journal is rich in detail. Pausch describes his men's journey across European borders from Germany and through the Netherlands to ships taking them across the Atlantic Ocean. It becomes even harder, once they arrive in America because all manner of supplies from transport to gunpowder must be approved by the English authorities. 'The National pride and arrogant conduct of these people,' Pausch laments in May 1777, 'allow them to command my men, while I am not permitted to command theirs!'

Disease and home-sickness afflicted the men under Pausch's command. 'Each of my men who was sent to the Hospital was not only afflicted with dysentery, but, as the hospital doctors told me, talked day and night of fathers, mothers, brothers, sisters, cousins, and aunts, besides, ... until they had to stop for actual want of breath! For this disease there is, as is well known, but one remedy in the world, viz: dear peace, and a speedy return [home], and with this hope I comfort my sick daily. With those still alive and well, I am perfectly satisfied; for they find plenty of solace in the Canadian girls and women. For this reason, ... they are happy and contented.'

Entering America from Canada, Pausch and his men were in the northern arm of an intended British pincer movement, the southern and western arms of which failed to materialise. Surrounded by American revolutionaries, they fought a heroic last stand near Saratoga, New York. Pausch's artillery fought effectively, despite the collapse of their infantry support, by firing canisters – containers full of lead shot which rained down on the enemy – instead of cannon balls. '[The enemy] pushed forward vigorously towards my cannons, in the hope of silencing them. This effort failed twice, and was prevented by firing canister. Two cart-loads of ammunition were fired by my cannons, and I had started on the third. My cannons were so hot that no one could place a hand thereon.'

The Hesse-Hanau artillery could not hold out forever and they were eventually captured as they tried to move to safer ground. Saratoga was a decisive victory for the Americans. Pausch was eventually repatriated to Hesse-Cassel where his name disappeared from regimental records in 1796.

ABOVE: A painting of the British surrender at Saratoga on 17th October 1777. This was considered a turning point in the American Revolutionary war which spurred the hopes of success in the American soldiers.

Nicholas Cresswell, English settler in the American colonies

(1750–1804)

'Edale – Tuesday, March 1st, 1774. I have been studying and deliberating for a long time how to shape my course in the world, and am this day come to a determined resolution to go into America, be the consequence what it will.'

Thus begins the diary of adventurous young Nicholas Cresswell, the son of a prosperous sheep farmer in the north of England. 'I am certain,' he continues, 'to meet with every possible obstruction from my parents and Friends, but I am resolved to brave them all and follow my own inclination for once.' Nicholas had recently met Kirk, the son of the village blacksmith, newly returned from the New World, with reports of the opportunities there for a young man prepared to work hard. As a man who grew up on an upland farm, he felt himself to be eminently qualified.

Cresswell landed in Maryland and made his way to Alexandria in Virginia. His encounters there with Indigenous people, enslaved people and fellow settlers are recorded with diligence and detail. Nicholas was no soft incomer. He traded and explored, living on the end of his means by wit. Preparing to head, against the advice of others, into 'Indian country' in August 1775 he fell in with John Anderson, a trader with the indigenous. 'Employed an Indian Woman to make me a pair of Mockeysons and Leggings,' he recorded. 'Mr. Anderson informs me that the Indians are not well pleased at anyone going into their Country dressed in a Hunting shirt. Got a Calico shirt made in the Indian fashion, trimmed up with Silver Brooches and Armplates so that I scarcely know myself.'

His observations are fascinating, and never more so than in expressing his views on the swelling anti-British sentiment among the longer-established settlers. He can see faults on both sides, but is especially critical of the fanatical puritanism which he believes is driving the coming rebellion. 'Committees are appointed to inspect into the Characters and Conduct of every tradesman,' he writes in October 1774, 'to prevent them selling Tea or buying British Manufactures. Some of them have been tarred and feathered, others had their property burnt and destroyed by the populace.'

He has first-hand experience of the hostility of the so-called Patriots. 'Wednesday, November 2nd, 1774. Writing to my Friends at home. Obliged to put the best side outwards and appear a little Whigified [in my choice of words], as I expect my letters will be opened before they get to England.' And 'Sunday, February 26th, 1775. No letters from home. I am afraid none will arrive, while the times are in such confusion. The rascals seize all Foreign letters.' Two days later, 'This is the last day Tea is allowed to be drank on the Continent, by an act of Congress. The ladies seem very sad about it.'

Cresswell's journal is a terrific record of its times, a relatively balanced view of the tensions between settler and native, and between colonist and coloniser. After three years of mixed fortunes brought on by bad luck and the disadvantages of being British, Nicholas Cresswell could take no more of the Patriots' dictatorial prejudice. War had by then broken out, and – denied the chance to serve his home country by the British governor of Virginia – Cresswell set sail for England. As he wrote on the eve of his departure, 'This country turned Topsy Turvy, changed from an earthly paradise to a Hell upon terra firma.'

LEFT: A portrait of Nicholas Cresswell in around 1780. He had travelled to America in 1774, aged twenty-four.

Eliza Fay, English traveller to India

(1740–1795)

A single woman trying to make her way in colonial India during the seventeenth and eighteenth centuries faced many obstacles. Throughout the trials and tribulations documented in her journals, Eliza Fay never gave up, and her love for her adopted country shines throughout her writing.

Eliza Fay, born Eliza Clement in Surrey, England, married Anthony Fay when she was only sixteen years old. He was a barrister with ambitions to practice law at the Supreme Court of Calcutta, and the couple travelled there in 1779. The journey was not uneventful: travelling through France not long before the French Revolution they met Marie Antoinette, and successfully evaded bandits in the deserts of Egypt. Landing at Calicut (modern-day Kozhikode) on India's Spice Coast they were held as political hostages by the King of Mysore for fifteen weeks. A Jewish merchant in Cochin (now Kochi) helped negotiate their release 'at last ... from a situation of which it is impossible for you to appreciate the horrors', and they eventually arrived in Calcutta in mid-1780.

All this Eliza wrote down in her journals and letters home, where she also noted that she was travelling to India primarily to keep an eye on Anthony, 'with a view to preserving my husband from destruction.' His 'dissipated habits,' she admitted, could lead to extravagance, argument, and 'violence of temper.' Mr Fay managed to have his name entered on the court roll, but failed to attract enough clients to sustain the couple. The marriage came under further strain when Eliza discovered 'a natural child of my husband's, whose birth had caused me bitter affliction.' The couple returned to England and formally separated in 1781.

Released from her marriage, Eliza is determined to make the most of her freedom, and several times she writes with pleasure of handsome young men. After breakfasting with one, twenty-three-year-old Captain Gibbon Pittman, 'one of the most elegant young men I ever saw,' they spend the day together, while 'he obligingly drove me in his Curricle round Waltair and shewed me Sardinia Bay, and several other spots remarkable for their beauty.' Unchaperoned, this was not ladylike.

She may have been done with Anthony, but she was not finished with India, to which she returned four times. In search of an income, Eliza returned to Calcutta and went into business as a milliner. She was, alas, no more successful than her husband. A Trust Fund bailed her out on one occasion in 1788; on another, in 1793, she kept afloat only by selling her house; and a year later she auctioned off all her stock and property to raise the cost of a passage back to Britain.

Soon after Eliza's return, a scheme to export goods from Bengal to America in which she had invested was scuttled when the ship carrying her cargo caught fire and sank. Undaunted, she returned to Calcutta once again, 'affording the only chance of attaining independence, and ultimately securing a home in my native country.' She never achieved the security which she sought. Further attempts included the establishment of a school for young ladies and gentlemen in London which prospered for a while until she fell out with her business partner. With the help of a loan from the East India Company Eliza returned once more to Calcutta in 1814 and died there penniless a year later.

Her journal is an enjoyable narrative, full of well-expressed irritation, anger, happiness and pleasure. The diary is notable for its uncommon appreciation of India's population and customs. It was published posthumously in an effort to pay her debts and – too late for Eliza – achieved sales of over £200.

RIGHT A portrait of Eliza Fay in Egyptian costume.

ABOVE: A portrait of England-born Elizabeth Macarthur from an unknown artist.

Elizabeth Macarthur, Australian pastoralist and merchant

(1750–1804)

The daughter of an English farmer, Elizabeth Macarthur married an army officer and was the first soldier's wife to arrive in the young colony of New South Wales. Her diaries and letters are an intriguing record of early colonial life and her lasting contribution to New South Wales' economic sustainability.

Elizabeth and John Macarthur arrived with the Second Fleet, a convoy of British ships which landed settlers, convicts and supplies at Sydney Cove in 1790. The flotilla, sometimes known as the Death Fleet, is today notorious for the dreadful conditions on board its ships. A quarter of the convicts died en route and almost half the survivors arrived in such poor health that they were dead within six months of reaching Australia.

John was a violent man – he fought a duel with one of the ships' captains before it had even left England and was later arrested for injuring a fellow officer in another. He and his regiment ran a trading cartel in New South Wales, imposing a monopoly on liquor and convict labour which made them rich and earned the regiment the nickname of 'the Rum Corps'. John corruptly secured generous grants of land on which he established Elizabeth Farm. He exerted violent control over the colony's resources, and even arranged for his brother in England to supply the uniforms for his troops. Although subsequent governors of New South Wales attempted to rein in the power of the Rum Corps, the men staged a military coup known as the Rum Rebellion.

During this time, Elizabeth Macarthur, who could not have been ignorant of her husband's gangster-like activities, ran the farm. Her sheep-rearing skills led to the development of merino wool, the export of which made both Macarthur and New South Wales rich. Eliza's collected journals and correspondence begin with her departure from England in 1789 and end in 1839, five years after John's death when she successfully took over control of his business interests, by then mostly legitimate. The Macarthurs had seven children and her frequent letters to them, often written over several days, are akin to diaries.

In one letter to her son Edward in 1830, Elizabeth reports an all-too-common recent event: '[Mr McAlister] has had a narrow escape in a Skirmish with a desperate set of Bush rangers in which he was wounded, but not severely – one of the mounted police under his command was also wounded – and a Constable severely so – the desperados were all finally Captured – tried at Bathurst and Executed – there are a few men out here committing depredations on the most frequented roads, in broad and open day light.'

The same letter contains early concerns for John's health as she writes 'he is still very low – he goes not out – but yet I am convinced it is not bodily ailment – altogether Hypochondria.' A year later she reports 'your father looking well, but still labouring under great depression of spirits.' By the end of 1831 'your poor father – after a severe paroxysm of suffering is now, I trust, in a way to be relieved – his mind begins to right itself.'

In 1832 John was declared insane and confined to Elizabeth Farm, where he died two years later. 'I had fondly indulged myself with the hope,' she wrote after his burial, 'that it would have pleased God to restore the dear departed to a more sane state of mind – that he was restored to reason for a few minutes I have no doubt – more was not granted.'

John Quincy Adams, 6th President of the United States of America

(1767–1848)

John Quincy Adams' father, second President of the USA and a committed diary keeper, advised his son to do likewise. The journal, which the future sixth president kept from the age of twelve for almost seventy years captures his eloquence, wisdom and progressive passion.

Politicians of every stripe have kept diaries through the ages – sometimes as a record of government; sometimes as a place to vent their own frustrations; sometimes for private, personal introspection; and often with a view to publication and self-justification. John Quincy Adams kept his, at first because his father recommended it and then out of habit. It was a place for reflection upon the day and for ordering his thoughts on the issues of tomorrow.

Adams is considered one of, the finest diplomats and statesmen of American history. He learned the skills at his father's knee, travelling with Adams senior from an early age on postings to France, the Netherlands and Russia. He returned to the Netherlands as the US ambassador in 1794, and subsequently held similar posts in Portugal and Prussia; and in 1809 he was appointed US Minister to Russia by President Madison, where he witnessed Napoleon's disastrous invasion of Russia. Adams negotiated a far better peace treaty with Great Britain after the War of 1812 than the British would have liked.

Elected president in 1824, he had a frustrating time in office. John's ambitious and progressive programs were thwarted by the emergence of America's polarising two-party political system during his presidency, which promoted discord over consensus. Despite failing to be re-elected for a second term John believed there was still work to be done, and served in the House of Representatives for nine terms, until his death. In this position he campaigned for the rights of enslaved peoples, women and America's Indigenous population. In 1789 John was already acutely aware of the cultural differences between the northern and southern states, writing, 'difficulty of adjusting the opposing sentiments which direct the conduct of men living in different climates and used to very different modes of living.'

In adult life, John Quincy Adams witnessed not only the birth of America but the government of its first eleven presidents. His diaries contain detailed accounts of the young nation's history, written with the descriptive colour and eye for character of an accomplished novelist, rather than a politician. John's acute powers of observation are apparent from an early age. He was not one to be overawed by those who might have expected his respect as his elders, if not betters. As he wrote on September 17th 1789 of sometimes presidents James Madison and Andrew Jackson: 'I attended this morning in the gallery of the house of representatives; to hear the debates. They were upon the judiciary bill. Mr. Gerry, Mr. Jackson, Mr. Burke, Mr. Stone, Mr. Lee, Mr. Maddison, & Mr. Benson all took a part in this debate. But I confess, I did not perceive any extraordinary powers of oratory display'd by any of these gentlemen. The subject had been already so much discussed, that little could be said of further importance. The eloquence had all been exhausted, but the spirit of contention still remained.'

Adams himself spoke so well that he acquired the nickname Old Man Eloquent and many hold his diaries to be the written embodiment of that quality.

ABOVE An daguerreotype of John Quincy Adams by Mathew Brady, taken one year before his death.

Sir Walter Scott, Scottish author

(1771-1832)

'I have all my life regretted that I did not keep a regular [journal]. I have myself lost recollection of much that was interesting and I have deprived my family and the public of some curious information by not carrying this resolution into effect.'

Thus wrote the historical novelist Sir Walter Scott on Sunday 20th November 1825. Scott had been introduced to Samuel Pepys' diary for the first time four months earlier and been enchanted by it. This, and a transcript of Lord Byron's diary which he read later in the year, inspired him to begin his own diary on that November Sunday.

Many readers regard Scott's diary as his greatest work – this, of a man who wrote *Ivanhoe*, *Rob Roy*, *Kenilworth* and the rest of the *Waverley* novels. Scott's fictional work had a lasting impact on the development of the novel in both Britain and America; but it is through his journal that he reveals himself. As his opening statement shows, Scott always intended the diary to be read by others; yet he eschews the dense narrative style of his popular fiction in favour of simpler, more personal expression.

On the second day, 21st November, he noted, 'I am enamourd of my journal. I wish the zeal may last.' It did. He kept this diary for the last seven years of his life; the final entry, five months before his death, ends in mid-sentence. Like all enthusiastic journal keepers, he picked out a special notebook in which to write: 'Behold I have a handsome locked volume such as might serve for a Ladies album.' The album remained on the shelves of his home, Abbotsford, in southern Scotland for seventy years after his death, until the American financier JP Morgan bought it. By then it had been published for the first time in 1890, and in the twenty-first century rests in New York's Morgan Library.

Scott was fifty-four when he began the journal, and it documents the old age of a famous and successful man. He records the tribulations of later life – the death of his wife, and the strokes which afflicted his final years – as well as the simple joys. Not long after those first entries the diary also charts the disastrous collapse of his publishers, in which he had a significant financial stake, and his determination to pay off his debts through hard work rather than declare bankruptcy. Scott wrote seven novels in the period covered by the journal, and at a time when he should have been enjoying a gentle retirement he remarked that 'I have become a sort of writing automaton.'

The burden of enforced work and his own physical decline took its mental toll too. He was prone to gloomy moods – what he described as 'the cold sinkings of the heart' – and mused on their nature. 'Is it the body brings it on the mind, or the mind inflicts it upon the body? ... I fancy I might as well enquire whether the fiddle or the fiddlestick makes the tune.'

Sir Walter Scott was a public figure, and his diary notes the many famed visitors. He remained a man of simple pleasures including long walks through the Selkirkshire countryside which cheered him enormously, describing 'the freshness of the air, the singing of the birds, the beautiful aspect of nature, the size of the venerable trees'. Of the grand dinners which he was obliged to host or attend, he wrote, 'I wish for a sheep's head and a whisky-toddy against all the French cookery and Champagne in the world.'

LEFT: An 1810 portrait of Sir Walter Scott.

Dorothy Wordsworth, English poet

(1771–1855)

Too often described first as William Wordsworth's sister and only second as a fine author in her own right, Dorothy Wordsworth wrote for the pleasure of writing rather than for cathartic release or public acclaim. Her journals were intended solely for the entertainment of her brother and a few choice friends.

Dorothy's journalling was compulsive, and often a record of a particular journey or sojourn. Travel stimulated her. Sometimes she would revise her notes later, as in the case of her *Recollections of a Tour Made in Scotland*, which she kept 'for the sake of a few friends, who, it seemed, ought to have been with us.' William and Dorothy's then-fashionable tour of Germany was recorded in her *Hamburgh Journal*; and there are further journals covering a tour of Switzerland and a second trip to Scotland.

Brother and sister lived in Dove Cottage in Grasmere, a village in England's Lake District for many years before and after William's marriage to his wife, Mary. The high mountains, valleys and lakes of the area were the epitome of the untamed nature which inspired William Wordsworth and his fellow Romantic Poets. Samuel Taylor Coleridge, Robert Southey, Charles Lamb and Sir Walter Scott were all visitors to Dove Cottage during the three-year period in which she kept her *Grasmere Journals*.

Both Dorothy and William had moved frequently around England and it was only at Dove Cottage that they began to feel settled and comfortably at home. Dorothy began her *Grasmere Journals* in 1800 when William went away for a short spell, intending that he should read it on his return to catch up on the daily life which he had missed.

In the end, it ran to five notebooks and one of the most interesting aspects of it is the central role which she played in her brother's poetry. Dorothy was a sharp and detailed observer of the world around her, both social and natural. Coleridge commented on the depth and range of her knowledge: 'her information various—her eye watchful in minutest observation of nature.' She wrote poetry too, but the prose of her journals is as rich as, sometimes richer than, her brother's verses.

William clearly drew inspiration from her use of language. For example, in the April 15th 1802 entry of her *Grasmere Journal*, she describes a walk that she and William took: 'I never saw daffodils so beautiful they grew among the mossy stones about and about them, some rested their heads upon these stones as on a pillow for weariness and the rest tossed and reeled and danced and seemed as if they verily laughed with the wind that blew upon them over the lake, they looked so gay ever glancing ever changing.' Two years later, William wrote his famous poem *I Wandered Lonely as a Cloud*, whose lines include:

'When all at once I saw a crowd,
A host, of golden daffodils;'

and

'Ten thousand saw I at a glance,
Tossing their heads in sprightly dance.'

It is as if William sometimes saw the world through Dorothy's eyes.

ABOVE: A portrait of Dorothy Wordsworth, sister of William Wordsworth and poet in her own right.

ABOVE: *An engraving of Napolean Bonaparte speaking with female contemporaries — showcasing an interaction not dissimilar to when Anna met him in 1807.*

Anna Tyszkiewicz, Polish noblewoman

(1779–1867)

The Age of Revolution in Europe, between the French Revolution of 1789 and a series of uprisings in several countries in 1848 was a time of great instability across the continent. Napoleon Bonaparte was responsible for much of it as he rampaged across Europe, transforming the French Republic into the First French Empire.

Napoleon was eventually brought to heel in substantial defeats at Moscow in 1812 (celebrated in Tchaikovsky's Overture of the same name) and at Waterloo in 1815 (also celebrated in music, by Abba). Until then however he appeared unstoppable, and the 1806 victory against Prussia at the Battle of Jena handed him the keys to Berlin. Less than a month later Napolean's troops marched into Warsaw, to the delight of that city's residents, who had been under hated Prussian rule.

One of those residents gleefully captured the moment in her journal. 'How shall I describe the enthusiasm with which it was received?' wrote Anna Tyszkiewicz, countess of Potocka, on November 21st 1806. 'This handful of warriors ... seemed to us a guarantee of the independence we were expecting at the hands of the great man whom nothing could resist.'

Anna was a Polish noblewoman of Lithuanian birth. She kept a diary between 1794 and 1820, witnessing Napoleon's rise and fall and many changes in her own life. She married the Count Potocki in Vilnius 1805 and divorced him in 1821. The disappointment of that may have been why she stopped writing. By then the Duchy of Warsaw, a puppet state established by Napoleon in 1808, had fallen to imperial Russia whose tsar Alexander I appointed himself its king.

The countess was an excellent recorder of history, from her privileged perspective. Her diaries give an insight into aristocratic life, with its grand balls, journeys through the constantly shifting political landscape of the times and connections to the highest authorities of her world. She was descended from Stanislaus Augustus Poniatowski, the last Polish king of Poland; and her husband, Count Potocki was Napoleon's chamberlain.

Anna's description of her first meeting with Napoleon himself is charming. She lived to the age of 91, but in the winter of 1807 Anna was a young woman, completely overawed by the charisma of the self-styled emperor, as she freely admitted. The occasion was a ball at which he was to meet the ladies of Warsaw, and she chose her wardrobe carefully – national pride was at stake. 'I wore a black velvet gown, attached à la Mathilde with gold and pearls. An open Van Dyke ruff, light tufts of curls, and all my diamonds matched this dignified and severe costume to perfection.'

She stood in line, waiting to be introduced as Napoleon made his entrance. 'M. Talleyrand advanced, with a loud and intelligible voice uttering the magic word that made the world tremble: "The Emperor." Immediately Napoleon made his appearance, and halted for a minute as if to be admired.' Anna was dumbstruck in his presence, like a pop fan in the orbit of her idol. 'I experienced a sort of stupor, a mute surprise. ... It seemed to me that he wore an aureole.' When her turn came to be presented, 'I cannot repeat what he said, so upset was I. ... I must no doubt have answered quite clumsily, for he looked at me with some surprise, which ... drove everything out of my mind except the gracious and gentle smile with which he accompanied the few words he said to me.'

Amhlaoibh Ó Súilleabháin, Irish draper and teacher

(1780–1837)

A shopkeeper and teacher who lived all but nine years of his life in the same Irish town, Amhlaoibh Ó Súilleabháin was actively involved in the campaigns for Catholic emancipation and the repeal of the Act of Union at a grassroots level. Both his political passion and enthusiasm for ornithology are illuminated within his diary.

Henry VIII of England, who broke the country's connection with Roman Catholicism in the sixteenth century, was declared King of Ireland in 1542. Thereafter Catholicism was suppressed in Ireland by several waves of English and Scottish Protestant ruling classes. James VI of Scotland filled the vacant throne of England in 1603 creating the United Kingdom of England, Ireland and Scotland. The Scottish and English parliaments merged in 1707, and in 1800 the Irish parliament joined them in a single parliament based in London.

Irish Catholicism has at several points in history been forced almost underground by Protestant legislation. Amhlaoibh Ó Súilleabháin (translated as Humphrey O'Sullivan) and his father had both been teachers in the so-called hedge schools which sprouted in Ireland in the eighteenth and early nineteenth century. Sometimes the schools met literally behind hedges, sometimes in discreet cabins, to teach the rudiments of the Catholic faith illegally and in secret. As Ó Súilleabháin wrote in his diary on February 3rd 1828, 'There is a lonely path near Uisce Dun and Móinteán na Cisi which is called the Mass Boreen. The name comes from the time when the Catholic Church was persecuted in Ireland, and Mass had to be said in woods and on moors, on wattled places in bogs, and in caves.'

His town, Callan in County Kilkenny, was a heartland of traditional Irish culture and language. Ó Súilleabháin wrote his diary in Gaelic, the native Irish language, and he was a collector of historic Gaelic manuscripts. These texts were often written in an archaic, highly formal version of the language, which occasionally appears in Ó Súilleabháin's diary entries.

Callan was, in the eighteenth century, almost three times the size it is today, with a degree of poverty to match. It was a breeding ground for resentment against the ruling authorities during the worst periods of anti-Catholic suppression. 'There is a large cave in Baile na Síg,' he noted on May 8th 1830, 'two miles west of Callan, which is called "The Rapparee's Hole." It seems they used to hide there after Cromwell's and King William's time. It's many the fine, good, honest man who had been reared in luxury and happiness who was reduced to robbery, begging, or exile by those two Englishmen.'

His diaries cover the years from 1827 to 1835 and he joyfully witnessed the passing of the Roman Catholic Relief Act of 1829 which was a milestone in the dismantling of religious, judicial and educational barriers to Catholic freedom throughout the United Kingdom. Politics aside, Amhlaoibh Ó Súilleabháin was a keen birdwatcher, and his diaries are full of nature notes.

He also found time for other leisure pursuits, although he did not always enjoy them. On September 11th 1830 he wrote a scathing review of one activity. 'Last Thursday in Dublin Castle I heard a band playing music which was like the music of Devils. The bassoons were like a sow crooning to her young. The musical pipe sounded like the squealing of piglets. The flute sounded like a muffled fart, the trumpets and French horns sounded like the laughter of fiends and the serpent like the sighing of demons, the trombone like the harsh cry of the heron. ... It in no way resembled the sweet, gently moving music of the Irish.'

ABOVE: A nineteenth-century depiction of Killarney in Ireland. Amhlaoibh's diaries recorded daily sights and events in a relaxed, conversational voice which help to paint a picture of everyday life in Ireland.

Thomas De Quincey, English man of letters

(1779–1867)

The future author of *Confessions of an English Opium Eater* kept a diary for only a few months in 1803, before he had begun to take the drug. Its pages witness the transformation of the solitary, introspective young Tom into the tortured, addictive poet.

Not all angst-ridden teenagers become poets; and not all poets are haunted by existential fears. Thomas De Quincey, however could be considered to fit the stereotype. His parents were intelligent but strict, especially his mother who raised him on her own after the death of his father when he was only eight. Thomas displayed a brilliant mind from an early age, to such an extent that his mother withdrew him from school for fear that he would become arrogant about it.

Poetry made a profound impression on De Quincey as a boy. He was infatuated with the works of William Wordsworth and Robert Southey, and he was in awe of Samuel Taylor Coleridge's *The Rime of the Ancient Mariner*. At the age of fifteen he was already adept enough to go to university but ran away instead, with the intention of travelling to Wordsworth's home in the Lake District, which was frequented by Southey and Coleridge.

Too young and anxious to undertake such a journey Thomas headed for Chester to see his sister. A sympathetic uncle persuaded him to try a more local adventure of walking through the Welsh countryside, on condition that he kept in touch with the family. He went "off-grid" however, living off berries for four months rather than returning home, then borrowed money to go to London, where family friends found him half-starved and brought him back to Chester.

De Quincey was then sent to Everton, near Liverpool, to recuperate. There he started to write a diary, which he kept up until he was admitted to Worcester College, Oxford later in 1803. He had spent, an unkind person might have said, far too much time on his own – indeed, he was described by someone who knew him at Oxford as 'a strange being who associated with no one'. His diary is inward-looking, as the entry for May 5th 1803 reveals: 'Last night I imagined to myself the heroine of the novel dying on an island of a lake, the chamber-windows (opening on a lawn) set wide open - and the sweet blooming roses breathing yr odours on her dying senses.'

The same day, there is more. 'Last night too I image myself looking through a glass. "What do you see?" I see a man in the dim and shadowy perspective and (as it were) in a dream. He passes along in silence, and the hues of sorrow appear on his countenance. Who is he? A man darkly wonderful - above the beings of this world; but whether that shadow of him, which you saw, be ye shadow of a man long since passed away or of one yet hid in futurity, I may not tell you.'

Thomas' obsession with the Lake District poets remained undimmed. On June 15th he wrote, 'I just said - "My imagination flies, like Noah's dove, from the ark of my mind ... and finds no place on which to rest the sole of her foot except Coleridge - Wordsworth and Southey."' He began to take opium during his time at Oxford, where he failed to graduate because he, once again, ran away, this time on the day of his final exam. De Quincey at last met his heroes, and eventually lived for ten years in the house, Dove Cottage, where Wordsworth had lived in Grasmere. He remained an addict for the rest of his life, and his periods of highest use of opium coincided with his periods of greatest literary productivity.

LEFT : A portrait of Thomas de Quincey by Sir John Watson-Gordon.

Lord Byron, English poet and traveller

(1788–1824)

The deliberate cremation of Lord Byron's memoirs after his death, by his publisher John Murray and the Irish poet Thomas Moore to whom Byron had entrusted the manuscript in 1821, is still considered one of the most heinous literary crimes ever committed.

'When you read my Memoirs you will learn the evils, moral and physical, of true dissipation. I can assure you my life is very entertaining and very instructive.' Thus, the poet described the manuscript which he had left with Moore, whom he instructed not to publish until after Byron's death.

Byron's life was as short as it was sensational, following the instant success which befell him after the publication by Murray of his epic poem *Childe Harold's Pilgrimage* in 1811. 'I awoke one morning,' he later recalled, 'and found myself famous.' He was twenty-four, and it seemed that fame went to his head. Byron lived a life of conspicuous, dissolute sexual promiscuity which damaged his reputation so comprehensively that he had to flee England in 1816 for fear of being lynched. He spent the rest of his life in southern Europe and died of a fever while fighting against the Ottoman Empire.

His memoirs, which covered the period to 1820, were burned; and details of his sexuality suppressed by his publisher, John Murray, for over a century for fear of further damaging his reputation and of the scandal which might engulf those named in them. However, four diaries did survive: one written while Byron was still in London, between 1813 and 1814; another describing a tour of Switzerland in 1816 which he gave to his sister; the *Ravenna Journal*, kept during his sojourn in that mosaic city in 1821; and a final record, the *Cephalonia Journal* which includes his last, thirty-sixth birthday on the Greek island of Kefalonia.

Byron was in Ravenna to pursue his love affair with the Contessa Guiccioli. She was nineteen, he thirty-one, and her husband sixty-nine. So far, so very Byronesque: however Byron was beginning to tire of his hedonistic lifestyle. On January 6th 1821, he compared his boredom in Ravenna with similar low spirits in his youth. 'What is the reason that I have been, all my lifetime, more or less ennuyé? and that, if any thing, I am rather less so now than I was at as far as my recollection serves? ... Temperance and exercise, which I have practiced at times, and for a long time – together vigorously and violently, made little or no difference. Violent passions did; – when under their immediate influence – it is odd, but, I was in agitated, but not in depressed spirits.'

He found that a dose of salts lifted his spirits like champagne, 'but wine and spirits make me sullen and savage to ferocity – silent, however, and retiring, and not quarrelsome, if not spoken to. Swimming also raises my spirits, – but in general they are low, and get daily lower. That is hopeless: for I do not think I am so much ennuyé as I was at nineteen. The proof is, that then I [had to] game, or drink, or be in motion of some kind, or I was miserable. At present, I can mope in quietness; and like being alone better than any company – except the lady's whom I serve.'

ABOVE: A portrait of the scandalous Lord Byron by Thomas Phillips, completed a year before the poet's death.

ABOVE: A French oil painting of Napoleon I on horseback with the smoke of the battlefield behind him. Despite various defeats Napolean is considered one of the greatest miliatary tacticans in history.

Jakob Walter, German soldier in the Napoleonic Wars

(1788–1864)

Jakob Walter was lucky to be alive. Of the 650,000 soldiers in Napoleon's Grande Armée which invaded Russia, only 30,000 – less than 0.5% - made it back. 200,000 were taken prisoner, and 420,000 soldiers died. Few were literate, and fewer still had time to write a diary of the horrors of war.

Walter's is one of only two surviving diaries of Napoleon's disastrous Russian campaign kept by ordinary soldiers; the other is by Jospeh Abbeel, a Belgian conscript. Walter was German, a stonemason by profession. He had been conscripted in 1806 into a Württemberg regiment which was loaned to Napoleon, at first for campaigns in Poland and Austria and then for the assault on Russia.

The vast majority of surviving journals from the period were written by the upper echelons of society: members of the landed gentry on whom war and its outcomes had political and financial impact. As a conscripted foot soldier, Jakob Walter had no such skin in the game and no great interest in who his commanders were or even whose side he was on – he barely mentioned Napoleon Bonaparte in his pages.

His everyday actions were driven by obedience to his immediate superiors and by self-preservation. The greatest threat to the latter was hunger and thirst, and Walter wrote at one point that most soldiers died of a lack of decent drinking water. Napoleon's great failing in the Russia campaign came from a lack of logistical support. Despite his well-known maxim that an army marches on its stomach, there was no planning for the supplies which an army might need, deep in enemy territory and far from home.

Many entries in Walter's diary deal with the need to find food, and the measures which soldiers were reduced to in order to eat. Sometimes they survived on looted flour mixed with muddy water and on one occasion he found a jar of honey which had been hidden by a Russian peasant and lived on that for a week. On another occasion, Walter collected the blood of a horse which had been shot, then '[I] set this blood on the fire, let it coagulate, and ate the lumps without salt.'

His perspective on war, seen from the battlefield rather than the distance heights of command is sobering. The assault on the city of Smolensk was a chaotic affair, Walter writes 'my company's doctor, named Staüble, had his arm shot away in crossing the stream, and he died afterward. Everyone fired and struck at the enemy in wild madness, and no one could tell whether he was in front, in the middle, or behind the centre of the army.'

Despite Walter's vivid descriptions, the things he saw desensitized him. One entry tells of how, while searching for a place to sleep one wintry night, Walter found a patch of softer ground on which to lay his head. The next morning he realised that he had been sleeping on the belly of a dead man which hadn't yet frozen solid.

Walter escaped the conflict with his life, no more than a limp and some occasional headaches. He raised a large family and wrote up his diaries as a unique memoir, which he posted in 1856 to his son Albert, who had emigrated to America. Albert had no idea of the true nature of the war his father had fought in; and without reading Jakob's diary, neither do we.

Anne Lister, English landowner, diarist and lesbian

(1791–1840)

Anne Lister's was a diary in two parts, and two alphabets. She wrote about her business and household affairs in plain English; but her love life and her innermost thoughts she recorded in a secret code of her own devising, and with good reason. Much of it was taboo.

'What a comfort my journal is,' Anne wrote on April 29th 1832. 'How I can write in crypt all as it really is and throw off my mind and console myself. I thank God for it.'

One might wonder what she would make of our fascination with her now that her "crypthand", as she called it, has been decoded. Perhaps Anne would be pleased to know we are a more liberal society in our attitudes to homosexuality. Yet, many of us still expose such vulnerabilities to our diaries in order to keep them hidden from the public.

Anne kept a diary from the age of fifteen until her early death from an insect bite when she was forty-nine. She journalled compulsively and her collected notebooks contain nearly five million words, expressing freely and forthrightly her dealings, and her feelings toward those she dealt with.

She was a successful and hard-nosed businesswoman who fought running battles with the businessmen with whom she had to contract in the Yorkshire town of Halifax. After one particularly satisfying victory, the outcome of which she noted in English on Christmas Eve 1832, she added in code, 'Mr R[awson] said he was never beaten but by ladies and I had beaten him. Said I gravely "is the intellectual part of us that makes a bargain, and that has no sex, or ought have none."'

Anne was a lesbian. Her sexuality, although not uncommon, was unacceptable in Victorian society. She was fully comfortable with her preferences, and although she was not "out" she dressed in mainly black without any feminine frills, a look which acquired her the nickname, Gentleman Jack. The encoded parts of Anne's diary conceal from prying eyes the details of her many affairs and the seduction of Ann Walker, who became the love of her life. On October 4th 1832, for example: 'I had my arm on the back of the sofa, she leaned on it, looked as if I might be affectionate and it ended in her lying on my arm all the morning and my kissing her and her returning it with much a long continued passionate or nervous mumbling kiss that we got on as far as we, by daylight, mere kissing, could - I thinking to myself: "Well, this is rather more than I expected."' Ann Walker's own diary was discovered in 2020.

Anne's easy ability to beat men at their own game, as the men perceived it, whether in business or in relations with women, made her many enemies. On one occasion a ruffian was hired to assault her. She recorded the incident in code, with some amusement.

'25th November 1832. An impertinent fellow with a great stick in his hand asked if I was going home and made a catch at my queer [private parts]. "Goddam you", said I, and pushed him off. He said something which I took as meaning an attack, so said I: "If you dare I'll soon do for you" and he walked one way and I the other. I did not feel the least frightened. How involuntarily and bitterly I always swear on these occasions!'

ABOVE: Anne Lister, often referred to as "the first modern lesbian".

ABOVE: A portrait of Shakespearean actor William Macready, a great thespian of his time. Macready's popularity waned as ordinary Americans began to favour home-grown talent over imported performers, who carried a whiff of colonial exceptionalism about them.

William Macready, English actor

(1793–1873)

William Macready was the greatest Shakespearean actor of his age. He reformed theatrical practice by insisting on rehearsals and going back to the original published texts of Shakespeare's plays, which had been badly mistreated by seventeenth- and eighteenth-century producers.

Macready made three tours of America during his career. America still regarded Shakespeare as the highest form of drama. It was said that gold miners in the Klondike used to entertain themselves of an evening by performing Shakespeare for each other by memory and in the upper levels of American society, English Shakespeareans such as Macready were considered the best interpreters of his work.

Macready's greatest rival in this respect was Edwin Forrest, born in Philadelphia and the younger of the two men. The two actors came to represent not only their own contrasting styles of acting but elements of class struggle and a lingering mistrust between Britain and America, which had prompted the American War of Independence seventy years earlier. Forrest took to staging the same plays as Macready, in the same towns and at the same time as the Englishman, inflaming the strong feelings of their audiences.

Things came to a head in Manhattan in May 1849. Supporters of Forrest bought up tickets for Macready's *Macbeth* at the Astor Place Theatre, a venue with a dress code, unlike the Broadway Theatre in which Forrest's Macbeth was being presented. As a shaken Macready recorded on May 7th, the barracking brought the play to a halt. 'They would not let me speak. They hung out placards – "You have been proved a liar," etc. ; flung a rotten egg close to me. ... Copper cents were thrown, some struck me, four or five eggs, a great many apples, nearly – if not quite – a peck of potatoes, lemons, pieces of wood, a bottle of asafoetida which splashed my own dress, smelling, of course, most horribly. ... At last a chair was thrown from the gallery on the stage, something heavy was thrown into the orchestra (a chair) which made the remaining musicians move out.'

The performance was abandoned and Macready determined to sail for England on the next boat but was dissuaded. On May 10th, 'I went, gaily, I may say, to the theatre, and on my way, looking down Astor Place, saw one of the Harlem cars on the railroad stop and discharge a full load of policemen; there seemed to be others at the door of the theatre. I observed to myself, "This is good precaution."' Forrest's mob had again filled the theatre and made their presence heard. During the first act they were forcibly evicted but then a crowd of around 10,000 of Forrest's friends who had been prevented from entering the Astor Place Theatre began to riot. 'Stones were hurled against the windows in Eighth Street, smashing many; the work of destruction became then more systematic; the volleys of stones flew without intermission, battering and smashing all before them.'

Audience and cast feared for their lives. Macready slipped out through a side door in disguise, while six hundred police and troops tried to control the well-orchestrated riot. Shots were fired, and in the aftermath (all vividly described in his diary by Macready) thirty-one people were found to have been killed, with more than 120 injured. As Macready prepared to flee the city in the early hours of the next morning, he heard an omnibus driving 'furiously down the street, followed by a shouting crowd. [A friend] asked the men pursuing, "What was the matter?" and one answered, "Macready's in that omnibus ; they've killed twenty of us, and by G we'll kill him!"'

Patrick Breen, American member of The Donner Party

(1795–1868)

The stream of pioneer settlers heading west on the Oregon Trail became a flood in the 1840s. One wagon train, composed mainly of members of the families of James Reed and George Donner, took an ill-advised short-cut and became trapped for four months by a vicious Sierra Nevada winter.

Reed was a first-generation Irish immigrant; Donner was a Kentuckian by birth. Their nine wagons were part of a larger convoy of around 500, and as the journey progressed they formed a group of around fifty with other families including that of Patrick Breen, another Irishman. At the Little Sandy River, the conventional route headed north to circumvent the Great Salt Lake. The Donner-Reed party however opted for the Hastings Cut-Off. This supposed short-cut, which actually added more than a hundred miles to the trail, was a route promoted by Lansford Hastings (who, despite having written about it in his book *The Emigrants' Guide to Oregon and California* had never travelled any part of it with a wagon) and Jim Bridger (who stood to profit because he ran a small supply depot along the way).

Without a guide, the Hastings route was difficult to find and dangerous to navigate compared to the well-trodden Oregon Trail. The crossings of the Wasatch mountain range and the dry Great Salt Lake and Desert beyond took far longer than expected, taking their toll on morale and supplies. Wagons were damaged; and cattle, which pulled the wagons and provided meat, died without water and grass.

Disagreement and delays meant that the Donner party arrived at the Sierra Nevada just as winter arrived. They pressed on, but heavy snow hid the route and the terrain from them and by November 4th 1846, when a blizzard began which lasted more than a week, they were forced to accept that they would have to winter near the pass they were trying to cross. Patrick Breen began to keep a diary on November 20th: 'we now have killed most part of our cattle having to stay here untill next spring & live on poor beef without bread or salt.'

The suffering was enormous, as the families endured some of the harshest winter conditions in North America. Food soon ran out and the group were reduced to boiling bones and chewing the rawhide from clothing, rugs and the roofs of their hastily and inadequately built log cabins. Time and again attempts to go for help were turned back by snow up to twenty feet deep. As the deaths began to mount, survivors turned to human flesh for sustenance, sometimes after murdering their victims. Patrick Breen wrote on February 23rd: '... shot Towser today & dressed his flesh Mrs Graves came here this morning to borrow meat dog or ox they think I have meat to spare but I know to the Contrary they have plenty hides I live principally on the same.'

Three separate rescue attempts reached the survivors in March 1847: 'there has 10 men arrived this morning from bear valley with provisions we are to start in two or three days & [Cache] our goods here there is amongst them some old they say the snow will be here untill June.' George Donner died four days before help arrived. The Breens and the Reeds were the only families to lose none of their family; and the Reeds claimed to be the only family not to have eaten any of their fallen comrades.

RIGHT: An extract from Patrick Breen's diary, displaying his distinctive cursive writing.

Thurs.d 25th { froze hard last
night fine & sunshiny
to day wind W. Mrs Murphy
says the wolves are about to
dig up the dead bodies at her
Shanty, the nights are too cold
to watch them, we hear them howl.

Frid 26th { froze hard last night to
day clear & warm Wind S:E: blowing briskly
Marthas jaw swelled with the toothache; hung-
ry times in camp, plenty hides but the folks
will not eat them we eat them with
a tolerable good apetite. Thanks be
to Almighty God. Amen
Mrs Murphy said here yesterday
that thought she would commence
on Milt. & eat him. I dont that she
has done so yet, it is distressing
The Donnos told the California folks
that they commence to eat the dead
people 4 days ago, if they did not
succeed that day or next in findi
ng their cattle under ten or
twelve feet of snow & did not know
the spot or near it, I suppose
they have done so ere this time

ABOVE: A water-colour portrait of Marjorie completed in 1811, the year she died aged only nine years old.

Marjorie Fleming, Scottish child diarist

(1803–1811)

The diary of a young girl takes the form of an exercise book. She was required to fill one page a day to practice her handwriting – although not, apparently, her spelling – and the entries are a mixture of that day's literary and religious lessons alongside her own impressions of people and places.

Marjorie Fleming grew up in southern Scotland, in the town of Kirkcaldy and the capital city of Edinburgh. She began to write when she was six and the journal ends with her untimely death from meningitis just short of her ninth birthday. It is a charming record of an intelligent, precocious child discovering the world about her at an impressionable age.

Much of the diary is taken up with her parroting of religious morals which her cousin and teacher Isabella Keith has taught her. 'Yesterday,' she confesses one Monday (the pages are not dated), 'I behave extremely ill in Gods most holy church for I would never attand myself nor let Isabella attend which was a great crime for she often often tells me that when to or three are geathered together God is in the midst of them and it was the very same Divel that tempted Job that tempted me I am sure but he resisted satan though he had boils ... which I have escaped.'

Misbehaviour is a recurrent theme. One Wednesday, 'I confess that I have been more like a little young Devil thaen a creature for when Isabella went up the stairs to teach me religion and my multiplication and to be good and all my other lessons I stamped with my feet and threw my new hat which she made on the ground and was sulky and was dreadfully passionate but she never whipped me but gently said Marjory go into another room and think what a great crime you are committing and letting your temper giet the better of you.'

Although she admits her errors, she is fairly unrepentant about them. One of her later entries consists of having to write out repeatedly,

I have been a Naughty Girl
I have been a Naughty Girl

For all her pious repetition of the dangers of evil, the wickedness of sin and the temptations of the Devil, she exhibits a tomboyish fascination with the darker side of humanity. Twice she refers to the *Newgate Calendar*, a sensational collection of crime reports collected in the guise of moral education. 'The *Newgate Calender* is very instructive, Amusing,' she notes, '& shows us the nesesity of doing good & not evels.' And later, 'There is a book that is caled the *Newgate Calender* that contains all the Murders, all the Murders I say, nay all Thefts & Forgeries that ever were committed & fills one with horror & consternation.'

She delights, as she grows into a mature eight-year-old, in nature, and is excited by storms, which she describes in language which she must have acquired through her enjoyment of reading. 'The trees do wave their lofty heads,' she imagines, 'while the winds stupenduous breath wafts the scattered leaves afar off besides the dedifities of the rocks leaves that once was green and beautifull now withered and all wed away scatering their remains on the footpaths and highroads.' No wonder Mark Twain said of Marjorie, 'She was made out of thunder-storms and sunshine, and not even her little perfunctory pieties and shop-made holinesses could squelch her spirits or put out her fires for long.'

Ralph Waldo Emerson, American author and philosopher

(1803–1882)

Waldo Emerson was a leader of the Romantic Movement in America, which celebrated individuality over conformity. He was a Transcendentalist, and believed in the fundamental beauty and goodness of nature. His journals, which many considered his finest writing, demonstrate that philosophy in action.

Ralph Waldo Emerson, who used his middle name in everyday life, was ordained as a pastor in Boston's Second Church in 1829. His faith was severely shaken over the next seven years by the early deaths through illness of two brothers and his wife Ellen – the latter after only two years of married life. Two years after her death he embarked on a lengthy tour of Europe, meeting many of the finest minds of the age including John Stuart Mills, William Wordsworth, Samuel Taylor Coleridge and Thomas Carlyle, who became a lifelong friend.

In Paris, Emerson visited the Jardin des Plantes, a botanical garden which profoundly impressed him with the realisation that all plants were interconnected through the system of evolution. He began to reject religion; and rather than holding God to be separate from our earthly world he saw God in all living things – a pantheistic outlook closer to the beliefs of the ancient world than to Christianity.

Emerson first formulated his theory of transcendentalism in 1836 as a long essay entitled Nature and developed it through lectures which he gave, and then published, over the next decade or so. It is said that he gave over 1500 lectures in his lifetime, many of them forming the basis for his subsequent publications. He lived and wrote according to his beliefs, as his recollection of a very ordinary encounter on September 19th 1838 demonstrates:

'I found in the wood this afternoon the drollest mushroom, tall, stately, pretending, uprearing its vast dome as if to say, 'Well I am some thing! Burst, ye beholders! thou luck-beholder! with wonder.' Its dome was a deep yellow ground with fantastic, starlike ornaments richly overwrought; so shabby genteel, so negrofine, the St Peter's of the beetles and pismires. ... I touched the white column with my stick, it nodded like old Troy, and so eagerly recovered the perpendicular as seemed to plead piteously with me not to burst the fabric of its pride. ... So, after due admiration of this blister, this cupola of midges, I left the little scaramouch alone in its glory. Good-bye, Vanity, good bye, Nothing! Certainly there is comedy in the Divine Mind when these little vegetable self-conceits front the day as well as Newton or Goethe, with such impressive emptiness.'

Emerson made another lifelong friend in Henry Thoreau, a fellow Transcendentalist. One of the first questions Emerson had asked of the younger man upon meeting was, 'Do you keep a journal?', and Thoreau's subsequent diaries are as inspiring as Emerson's own. Emerson gave the eulogy at Thoreau's funeral in 1862 and often described him as his best friend. Emerson frequently revealed his admiration for Thoreau in his diaries, as he did on July 18th 1852, extolling the virtues of what gardeners call weeds:

'Henry Thoreau makes himself characteristically the admirer of the common weeds which have been hoed at by a million farmers all spring and summer and yet have prevailed, and just now come out triumphant over all lands, lanes, pastures, fields, and gardens, such is their pluck and vigor. We have insulted them with low names, too, pig-weed, smart-weed, red-root, lousewort, chickweed. He says that they have fine names, amaranth, ambrosia.'

ABOVE: An 1857 daguerreotype of Ralph Waldo Emerson: essayist, philosopher, minister and poet.

George Sand, French writer

(1804–1876)

George Sand, born Amantine Lucile Aurore Dupin de Francueil, was the most popular writer in Europe for many years, outshining her countrymen Honoré de Balzac and Victor Hugo. A campaigning feminist, she outraged society with her scandalous liaisons, her masculine dress sense and male pen name.

Sand was a prolific author of plays, poetry and novels. Her first novel, *Indiana*, about a woman victimised by an abusive husband and an unreliable lover, was written a year after the failure of her marriage and shot her to fame in 1832. She embarked on a period of what she described as romantic rebellion, having affairs with actors, writers, and – most famously – a ten-year relationship with composer, Frédéric Chopin. Sand lived for a time in an apartment above that of another composer, Franz Liszt, of whom her journal notes, 'Franz's [Liszt's] piano is in a room on the ground floor under mine. My window, before which the lindens are swaying, is just above his window. ... I love those broken phrases which he flings from the piano, and which rest with one foot in the air, dancing off into space like little lame elves.'

She lived life to the full and very much in the present moment. Her journal was not a daily affair but an occasional tool in which to pour out thoughts and thereby order them. The result is a fresh, highly personal insight into Sand's mind and it is entirely appropriate that, when it was published in 1929 it was given the title *The Intimate Journal of George Sand.*

The journals are overwhelmingly life-affirming in tone. She had plenty of enemies, but in her pages there are only friends and colleagues. Sand suffered much mental anguish and in 1836 she was going through a period of despair from which she would emerge to begin her affair with Chopin. Addressing herself in her diary, she writes, 'When mental sickness increases until it reaches the danger point, do not exhaust yourself by efforts to trace back to original causes. ... Try to find the immediate daily causes of these crises. ... In that way you may prevent them, or at least diminish their force. When your mental state is normal, try to realize that the delirium is bound to recur. Then when you are delirious, strengthen yourself by the certainty that you will recover your mental poise.'

She had good cause on occasion to be down-hearted, but for Sand these moments are when she ponders instead the nature of happiness, particularly toward the end of her life. 'Maturity finds happiness in a state of grace,' she muses one day, 'that is, the consciousness of good behind one, before one, and within one. The capacity for such happiness shows complete absence of mean motives. In the state of grace one cannot bear to give pain or do injury. One need not be a saint or a great man, not even pose as virtuous in order to attain this state of being. It is within reach of everyone.'

Victor Hugo, one of her many literary admirers, gave the eulogy at George Sand's funeral. Referring to France's motto of liberty, equality and fraternity, he said that, 'being a part of the equality of men, a great woman was needed. It was necessary to prove that a woman could have all the manly gifts without losing any of her angelic qualities, be strong without ceasing to be tender ... George Sand proved it.'

LEFT: A photograph of George Sand dated to 1864, twelve years before her death.

Richard Wagner, German composer

(1813-1883)

Richard Wagner was admired for his ambitious "music dramas". While he preferred his operas to be known, he struggled all his life to balance the books. Wagner's love life was similarly chaotic, until he was given a handsome brown book, bound in leather and finished in gold and malachite trim – his new journal.

Wagner is notorious for his extravagant productions, which reflected his belief in Gesamtkunstwerk, a total work of art in which every element – scenery, music, libretto, costumes – played a full part in the whole. The effect, he intended, should be mind-blowing; indeed, as he wrote in 1859 to his former lover Mathilde during the composition of the opera *Tristan and Isolde*, 'I fear the opera will be banned ... only mediocre performances can save me! Perfectly good ones will be bound to drive people mad.'

By 1865 Richard had begun a new affair, with Cosima von Bülow, the wife of Hans von Bülow who conducted the premiere of *Tristan and Isolde* that year. Cosima had already borne Wagner a daughter, whom they named Isolde. Cosima was the illegitimate daughter of Franz Liszt, and her very public affair with Wagner scandalised society.

To complicate matters Wagner had another admirer in King Ludwig II, the so-called Fairy-Tale King of Bavaria. Ludwig was gay, and Wagner feigned interest in Ludwig's advances. The king settled the composer's large debts and sometimes invited Wagner to stay. On one occasion, two months after the premiere, Wagner was a guest at the king's mountain chalet, and wrote in his journal of his late-night arrival there:

'It was completely dark by the time I go up there far ahead of all the men, with a big bunch of keys to open the lodge. Luckily I got the last one to fit, tried to find my way about in the dark, found the King's sleeping place, and stretched out bathed in sweat, dog-tired. ... Completely in the wilds. No water to be found. Where is there a spring? We hadn't asked. Much groping about mountain and forest. In vain. Laborious changing of clothes - ah, what a muddle. Finally, bread, wine, sausage. But no water. So mineral water - brought for the cure - had to be unpacked. Arrival of good mood.'

Wagner always referred to his journal as 'the brown book' – to differentiate it from an earlier journal, 'the red book', which he had destroyed. The brown book was a gift from Cosima in 1865, to record events while he was apart from her. Despite Ludwig's feelings for Wagner, he had been forced to exile the composer from Munich in the wake of the scandal around the affair with Cosima.

The affair was however no passing fling. During another separation, in April 1867, he wrote, 'In my whole life I do not think I have ever been so sad as I am now!! - How easily that is said, and how unspeakable it is. ... I yearn for major illness and death. I have no inclination any more, no will!' Wagner's long-estranged wife had died fifteen months earlier, and Cosima was begging her husband for a divorce, which he refused. Hans finally conceded she had given birth to two more children with Richard – Eva, named after the heroine of *Die Meistersinger*, and Sigfried after the hero of *The Ring*.

Cosima was twenty-four years younger than Richard and outlived him by forty-seven years. She kept the brown book private for more than twenty years after his death; but in 1907 their daughter Eva presented it to the town of Bayreuth, where Wagner had first presented *The Ring* in 1876.

ABOVE: An image of Wagner in Munich, in 1871. Wagner was brought to the city by King Ludwig II who was admirer of his operas.

Henry David Thoreau, American author and philosopher

(1817–1862)

Henry Thoreau began to keep a journal in 1837 at the suggestion of his new friend Waldo Emerson. At first, subscribing to Emerson's nature-centred philosophy of Transcendentalism, Thoreau became increasingly political in his thoughts about the right to individuality of every person.

On October 22nd 1837, Henry Thoreau wrote of his meeting with Waldo Emerson: ' "What are you doing now?" he asked. "Do you keep a journal?" So I make my first entry to-day.' On June 24th 1863, a year after Thoreau's death, Emerson wrote:

'In reading Henry Thoreau's Journal, I am very sensible of the vigor of his constitution. That oaken strength which I noted whenever he walked or worked or surveyed wood lots, the same unhesitating hand with which a field-laborer accosts a piece of work which I should shun as a waste of strength, Henry shows in his literary task. He has muscle, and ventures on and performs feats which I am forced to decline. In reading him, I find the same thought, the same spirit that is in me, but he takes a step beyond, and illustrates by excellent images that which I should have conveyed in a sleepy generality.'

Thoreau is best known for his book *Walden*, a loosely autobiographical account of the two years, two months and two days which he spent in a woodland cabin by Walden Pond on land owned by Emerson. He built the cabin himself, and his time there, between 1845 and 1847, was an experiment in simplicity, individuality, personal development and self-sufficiency.

Halfway through his stay on Walden Pond, he was accosted by a tax collector who demanded six years of backdated poll tax payments. Thoreau refused on a matter of principle: he was opposed to the Mexican-American war on which many tax dollars were being spent. He spent a night in jail for his stance and was extremely annoyed to be released the following morning because an unknown benefactor had paid the tax bill, against his wishes.

The incident fed his belief in the right to self-determination, and by extension the right not to be governed by others. It prompted him to write a celebrated essay, *Resistance to Civil Government*, sometimes known as *Civil Disobedience*, in which he opined, 'I heartily accept the motto, "That government is best which governs least" ... Carried out, it finally amounts to this, which I also believe,— "That government is best which governs not at all."'

Thoreau was most interested in nature's relationship with humanity, and not with humanity itself. He read and subscribed to eastern religious philosophy and often seemed to actively distance himself from mankind, as through his stay at Walden Pond. He never married. And on April 2nd 1852 he wrote in his journal:

'I do not value any view of the universe into which man and the institutions of man enter very largely and absorb much of the attention. Man is but the place where I stand, and the prospect hence is infinite.'

LEFT: A nineteenth-century photograph of Henry David Thoreau, friend of Transcendentalist leader, Ralph Waldo Emerson.

Joseph Jenkins, Welsh-born Australian Swagman and self-educator

(1818–1898)

A successful Welsh farmer with a wife, nine children and a herd of prize-winning cattle, Joseph Jenkins walked away from it all at the age of fifty to begin a new life in Australia. His daily diary, which he kept for fifty-eight years, is now a standard teaching text in Australian schools.

Jenkins began to write a diary on New Year's Day in his twenty-first year, while he was still living at home on his father's farm. After his marriage, he bought the lease on a farm of his own which, through wise management and skill, was declared the best farm in the county of Cerdigion (Cardiganshire) in 1851. Jenkins advocated for several practices which are now widely accepted, such as fertilising fields with manure and rotating crops.

One night in 1868 his wife, three of their children and their maid assaulted him violently, which he believed was an attempted murder. He wrote on May 26th 1868 'my ribs and breastbone were fractured . . . I have an ugly black eye with about a dozen other different wounds'; and in later entries he often cited this as the reason for his abrupt departure for the Antipodes – 'it was not my fault I absented myself from home.' Jenkins suspected his wife of infidelity; and by 1868 he was drinking heavily and neglecting the farm.

Joseph left without notice and arrived in Melbourne in 1869, possibly inspired by two of his brothers who had earlier emigrated to Canada. He gave up alcohol and became a swagman, an itinerant farmhand who walked from place to place looking for work and carrying his belongings – his swag – on his back. A prolonged drought however made work scarce. Soon after his arrival he wrote, 'Unbearably hot with the temperature registering 118°F (48°C) ... Dreadful stench from the carcasses of dead sheep. ... The flies are troublesome; my face is swollen from mosquito bites. The cattle are bellowing for water and dying by the score; the stench is unbearable. The land looks more like scorched hearths than green fields.'

Desperate fellow swagmen, whom he called 'beggars, loafers and vagabonds', often tried to rob him of his bedding and other property. They stole his boots once, and two volumes of his diaries. He was no more impressed by the state of the countryside, for which he blamed aspirational parents: 'The two qualifications required of the young are dancing and piano-playing, not milking and butter- or cheese-making. Smeaton district, once considered the garden of Victoria, is now a ruinous area from continued exhaustion of the land. The farms are over-run by weeds. There are numerous deserted homesteads.'

Jenkins eventually felt he was too old for this lifestyle and managed to buy an acre of land and build a small cottage. He despised the large landowners who let fertile land go unattended. 'I met an Aborigine,' he wrote on 22nd July 1887. 'He seemed half starved. ... A few men in the colony own over a million acres of rich land which was barbarously taken from the Aborigines. The majority held it as of right and even a Christian obligation to be rid of all the Aborigines. In the name of everything – whence came such authority?'

At the age of seventy-six Jenkins felt the urge to return to his home country. He brought all his diaries with him and stored them in the attic of the family farm, where they were rediscovered seventy years later. As he once wrote, presciently, 'through this [diary] I am building . . . my own monument.'

ABOVE: Three photographs of Joseph Jenkins taken in 1871. Jenkins posted these images back home to Wales from Australia, to showcase his new life. The first image shows Jenkins as a "Swagman", the second as a rural farmer and the third as "a man of letters".

ABOVE: Queen Victoria's journals are stored in the Royal Archives at Windsor Castle. However, they were made widely available in 2012 at the behest of then reigning monarch, Elizabeth II.

Queen Victoria, English queen and empress

(1819–1901)

Until Queen Elizabeth II, Britain's Queen Victoria was by far the country's longest reigning monarch. She kept a personal diary throughout her life which, even in the form edited by her daughter Beatrice after her death, occupies 111 volumes – about a third of its original length.

The Victorian Era is often regarded as a golden age in British history, and the queen's diaries record both private and public moments throughout it. Under her reign, Britain was at the height of its industrial power and global influence, as well as Britain's colonial Empire at its greatest extent.

First begun at thirteen, and on June 20th 1837, when Victoria was eighteen she 'was awoke at 6 o'clock by Mamma. ... Lord Conyngham (the Lord Chamberlain) then acquainted me that my poor Uncle, the King [William IV], was no more, and had expired at 12 minutes past 2 this morning, and consequently that I am Queen. ... Since it has pleased Providence to place me in this station, I shall do my utmost to fulfil my duty towards my country; I am very young and perhaps in many, though not in all things, inexperienced, but I am sure, that very few have more real good will and more real desire to do what is fit and right than I have.' For the rest of the day, and of her reign, she displayed remarkable self-possession in her dealings with ministers and the business of state.

Victoria's description of the day of her coronation a year later is long and vivid. 'I was awoke at four o'clock by the guns in the Park,' she began, 'and could not get much sleep afterwards on account of the noise of the people, bands, etc.' Crowds lined the streets, and on her way to be crowned in Westminster Abbey 'their good humour and excessive loyalty was beyond everything, and I really cannot say how proud I feel to be the Queen of such a Nation.' At the moment of coronation, 'the Crown being placed on my head; - which was, I must own, a most beautiful impressive moment; all the Peers and Peeresses put on their Coronets at the same instant ... The shouts, which were very great, the drums, the trumpets, the firing of the guns, all at the same instant, rendered the spectacle most imposing.'

Not everything went according to plan. As the clergy and nobility queued to renew their allegiance to the Crown, 'poor old Lord Rolle, who is 82 and dreadfully infirm, in attempting to ascend the steps, fell and rolled quite down, but was not the least hurt; when he attempted to reascend them I got up and advanced to the end of the steps, in order to prevent another fall.' As part of the ceremony, the Archbishop of Canterbury traditionally places a ring on the fourth finger of the new monarch's hand, to symbolise the king's or queen's bond of devotion to the nation. But 'the Archbishop had put the ring on the wrong finger, and the consequence was that I had the greatest difficulty to take it off again, - which I at last did with great pain.'

Sixty years after her accession to the throne, the British Empire celebrated the queen's diamond jubilee, which she described as 'a never-to-be-forgotten day.' Over breakfast, she watched a parade of British and foreign troops passing her window, before proceeding to Buckingham Palace. 'My escort was formed from the 2nd Life Guards and officers of the native Indian regiments.' There she greeted the crowds and did something which would have been impossible at the start of her reign. 'Before leaving I touched an electric button, by which I started a message which was telegraphed throughout the whole Empire. It was the following: "From my heart I thank my beloved people, May God bless them!" At this time the sun burst out.'

Fyodor Dostoevsky, Russian novelist

(1821–1881)

Fyodor Dostoevsky's work epitomises the panoramic yet claustrophobic Russian novel of the nineteenth century. His diary was a public journal, written for a newspaper column (subsequently a book), called *The Diary of a Writer* in the last decade of his life.

Dosteovsky's books are profound fictional explorations of the human condition. *Crime and Punishment*, *The Idiot* and *The Brothers Karamazov* are often included in lists of the greatest novels ever written. The author himself rarely enjoyed success or financial security from these ventures and instead it was the articles in *Diary of a Writer* which brought him the most contemporaneous recognition. When the first compilation was published in book form, it sold twice as many copies as his previous novels. Tsar Alexander II insisted that Dostoevsky present him with a copy personally, which was ironic considering that Dostoevsky was under police surveillance for most of his life for his liberal attitudes.

Dosteovsky's is not a diary in the conventional sense of a record of daily events. It is however a reflection of the scope of the writer's interests and imagination. While one article might be an autobiographical recollection, another is a report on the latest sensational crime to scandalise the Russian public, another a short story, or the outline for a new novel. Sometimes he would write a comedy sketch, sometimes a portrait in words of a famous figure from the past, and occasionally a meditation on what the future might bring. The sheer variety of authorial voices, styles and references which Dostoevsky delivered for the *Diary* is staggering.

When it came to autobiography, Dostoevsky had a bone to pick. In an article from January 1876 entitled *A Word Apropos my Biography*, he wrote: 'The other day I was shown my biography printed in *The Russian Encyclopaedic Dictionary*. It is difficult to imagine that so many errors could have been crowded into half a page. I was born not in 1818, but in 1822. My late brother, Mikhail Mikhailovich, the editor of the magazines *Time* and *Epoch*, was my elder brother, and not my junior by four years.' It was an unfortunate start to the article: the editor of the dictionary may have been wrong, but so was Dostoevsky, who was born not in 1822 but in 1821.

He continued indignantly 'after the expiration of my term at hard labour, to which I was sent in 1849 as a state criminal (not a word is mentioned on the nature of my crime, and people might think that I was exiled for robbery)'. Dostoevsky preferred the truth about his being sent into exile, which was due to his membership of a literary group of progressive intellectuals organised by the socialist Mikhail Petrashevsky – 'after the term of my conviction, by the will of the Emperor, I was immediately inducted as a private [soldier, by conscription]. ... But I was never deported to Siberia.' Again, this is not absolutely true – his term of hard labour was served in Omsk, today the third largest city in Siberia. In another article he even described the conditions – 'Filth on the floors an inch thick ... We were packed like herrings in a barrel ... There was no room to turn around. From dusk to dawn it was impossible not to behave like pigs ... Fleas, lice, and black beetles by the bushel.'

Dostoevsky had still more complaints about the editor of the dictionary. 'The order of my literary works is mixed up. [And] there are pure fabrications. [My biography] asserts that I was editor of *The Russian World*. ... I declare that was never editor of the newspaper *The Russian World*; moreover, never did I have a single line printed in that esteemed publication.' That, at least, is true.

ABOVE: An 1872 portrait of Dostoyevsky. Perhaps unusually, he had conceived of his diary as one complete work from its conception.

ABOVE: An image of Mary Boykin and her husband, James Chesnut Jr, who served as a U.S. senator.

Mary Boykin Chesnut, American diarist

(1823–1886)

History is usually written by the winners of battles and wars. A diary kept by the wife of a Confederate soldier offers a rare glimpse of the American Civil War from the South's perspective. The entries, spanning 1861-1865, were 'intended to be entirely objective,' Chesnut began. 'My subjective days are over.'

Mary Boykin Chesnut hailed from the upper levels of Southern society. Her father was governor of South Carolina and she was educated at Madame Talvande's French School for Young Ladies in Charleston. When her father left politics he bought a large cotton plantation in Mississippi where he owned hundreds of enslaved people.

She married James Chesnut when she was seventeen. Her husband's family owned a plantation about five square miles in size, with around 500 enslaved people to work it. He was a successful lawyer before the war, and after South Carolina seceded from the Union he was an aide to the Confederate president Jefferson Davis and a brigadier-general in the Confederate Army. Mixing in such high circles, Mary was expected to be an entertaining and charming wife; and her wit and intelligence are apparent in her diaries. The diaries were published posthumously, but she prepared them for publication herself in the 1880s, retaining a marvellous narrative sense of not knowing what was going to happen next, to draw in her readership.

Mary's husband was charged with negotiating the surrender of the Unionist forces led by Colonel Robert Anderson which were occupying Fort Sumner in Charleston when war broke out. Writing on April 12th 1861, she reviewed the day. 'Mr. Chesnut returned. His interview with Colonel Anderson had been deeply interesting, but Mr. Chesnut was not inclined to be communicative. He wanted his dinner. He felt for Anderson and had telegraphed to President Davis for instructions.'

Mary's accounts read as if she recorded events simultaneous to them happening, and later the same day in 1861 she picked up her pen again. 'He has now gone back to Fort Sumter with additional instructions. If Anderson does not accept terms at four, the orders are, he shall be fired upon.' Another pause, then, 'I count four, St. Michael's bells chime out and I begin to hope. At half-past four the heavy booming of a cannon [from the besieging Confederate ships in the bay]. I sprang out of bed, and on my knees prostrate I prayed as I never prayed before.'

The historic significance of these first shots of the Civil War were not lost on Mary and her companions. Her initial relief is palpable. 'Do you know, after all that noise and our tears and prayers, nobody has been hurt; sound and fury signifying nothing - a delusion and a snare.'

But the cannon and the siege continued. Mary wrote in her diary on April 15th, 'I did not know that one could live such days of excitement. Someone called: "Come out! There is a crowd coming." A mob it was, indeed, but it was headed by Colonels Chesnut and Manning. ... They were escorted to Beauregard's headquarters. Fort Sumter had surrendered!'

Mary Chesnut was as good as her word in remaining objective, as proud of her husband as she is critical of the South's attitude to women and enslaved people. Her diary is a smart, lively account.

Barbara Bodichon, English educationalist, feminist and traveller

(1827–1891)

Barbara Bodichon was a member of the Langham Place Circle, one of the earliest feminist groups in modern history. She co-founded *The English Women's Journal*, which campaigned on women's issues; and she used her honeymoon in North America to make connections with activists on that continent.

Bodichon's is a name not often heard these days, but she was a powerhouse of feminist activism in her lifetime. She and kindred spirits began to meet at 19 Langham Place in central London in the 1850s and the building became a sort of antidote to the chauvinistic Gentlemen's Clubs of the period: eventually housing meeting rooms, a reading room and a coffee shop. It was from there that *The English Women's Journal* was published every month for six years from 1858 to 1864.

One of the group's early concerns was the unfairness of English Law in regard to the property of married women. The members formed a working group called the Married Women's Property Committee, and Bodichon compiled *A Brief Summary of the Laws of England concerning Women. The Summary* was published in 1854 and eventually contributed to the passing of the Married Women's Property Act in 1882, which made it legal for married women to own property in their own right for the first time.

Barbara Bodichon, born Barbara Leigh Smith, was one of five children. Her parents caused a scandal by never marrying, and she turned down her first suitor's proposal of marriage because to do so would have meant the loss of her legal rights. She wedded a French doctor, Eugène Bodichon, in July 1857, just a month before the passing of the Matrimonial Causes Act. The Ladies of Langham Place had campaigned for the legislation, which allowed women access to the divorce courts for the first time.

Barbara and Eugène spent their honeymoon in America so that she could collect information about the practices of slavery, and she kept a diary in the form of letters to her father, who had been a friend of the great English abolitionist William Wilberforce. Soon after her arrival in the country, she recorded a conversation in which she took part: '11 December 1857. Mr C. is reading a paper and read out loud the announcement of the marriage of a mulatto and a white girl; it excites from all expressions of the utmost disgust and horror. I say, "It is very uncommon?" Mr C. "Yes! thank God. Only permitted in Massachusetts and a few states." "There seems to be nothing disgusting in it. My brothers went to school with a mulatto and I with a mulatto girl." All: "At school! At school with niggers!" "Yes." All: "Horrid idea, how could you?" BLS [her own initials]: "Why, your little children all feel it possible to come in close contact with negroes, and they seem to like it; there is no natural antipathy." Some: "Yes, there is an inborn disgust which prevents amalgamation."'

She made time to visit Lucretia Mott, a Quaker, feminist and abolitionist, as her home in Pennsylvania, and was enchanted. '20 April 1858. She looks just like a picture. I never saw such a dress, like a pearl. I fell in love with her immediately. She looks "full of grace" in every sense of the word. I do not wonder her preaching has stirred so many souls, her aspect is eloquent, her smile full of good things. ... She put her hands on my shoulders and said how happy it made her to see that the young women of England were thinking about their rights and trying to do something for justice and freedom.'

ABOVE: Bodichon was well-travelled and well-versed. n her lifetime she met abolitionist Wendell Phillips as well as philosopher Ralph Waldo Emerson.

Leo Tolstoy, Russian novelist and social reformer

(1828–1910)

Tolstoy asked a lot of his journals. They were required to be at once records of the day's activity, challenges for tomorrow's and reviews of yesterday's; explorations of self, rules for living, and a place for confessions and self-flagellation. Past, present and future are accounted for on every page.

Author of *War and Peace* and *Anna Karenina*, Tolstoy kept a diary throughout his life from the age of eighteen, when he was being treated for a venereal disease, until he was close to death in 1910. His entries reveal a man driven by the need to improve himself and the society in which he lived – tasks for which he always berated himself for failing to achieve.

The diaries of his youth are full of self-recrimination. He was in the habit of drawing two columns for each day. In the first, he would lay out his plans for the day, as for example in this entry from March 25th 1851: 'From 10 to 11 yesterday's diary and to read. From 11 to 12 — gymnastics. From 12 to 1 — English. Beklemishev and Beyer from 1 to 2. From 2 to 4 — on horseback. From 4 to 6 — dinner. From 6 to 8 — to read. From 8 to 10 — to write. — To translate something from a foreign language into Russian to develop memory and style. — To write today with all the impressions and thoughts it gives rise to.'

The second he concluded the following day, to report on how successfully he had completed the previous tasks. Thus, reviewing on March 26th his intentions for the 25th he wrote:

'Awoke late out of sloth. Wrote my diary and did gymnastics, hurrying. Did not study English out of sloth. With Begichev and with Islavin was vain.
At Beklemishev's was cowardly and lack of fierté. On Tver Boulevard wanted to show off. I did not walk on foot to the Kalymazhnyi Dvor (sissiness). Rode with a desire to show off. For the same reason rode to Ozerov's.
— Did not return to Kalymazhnyi, thoughtlessness.
At the Gorchakovs' dissembled and did not call things by their names, fooling myself. Went to L'vov's out of insufficient energy and the habit of doing nothing.
Sat around at home out of absentmindedness and read Werther inattentively, hurrying.'

The stresses are consistent of Tolstoy. As if this harsh self-criticism were not enough, he also kept separate notebooks with titles such as *Journal for Weaknesses*, *Rules for Life*, *Rules for Developing Will*, and *Rules for Playing Cards in Moscow until January 1*.

It's hard to believe that he enjoyed any aspects of life: but even Tolstoy must have seen the light-hearted side to his entries such as the one from January 25th 1851. 'I've fallen in love or imagine that I have; went to a party and lost my head. Bought a horse which I don't need at all. Rules. Don't offer a price for a thing you don't need. On arriving at a ball, ask someone to dance at once and take a turn with her at a waltz or a polka. Think about ways of putting my affairs in order this evening. Stay at home.'

LEFT: Leo Tolstoy in Yasnaya Polyana, taken in 1908. His was the first colour photo portrait in Russia.

Emily Pepys, English child diarist

(1833–1877)

A direct descendant of the celebrated seventeenth-century diarist Samuel Pepys, Emily was the daughter of an English bishop, sister of a vicar and sibling of the wife of another vicar. She herself married a third vicar. Before all that, at the age of eleven, she wrote a charming diary.

Growing up in relatively wealthy ecclesiastical circles, Emily Pepys was confident, well-educated and articulate. Her family pronounced their surname "peppis" rather than "peeps". Emily's is in one sense a very ordinary young girl's diary – there are no dramatic events; she is happy; and comfortably off. But therein lies its very charm. Although her sources of entertainment and amusement may sometimes be different from ours, Emily's life is eminently recognisable to all of us who have ever been the same age as she was. And sometimes the jokes are the same; on August 21st, 'The servant came up and said "Your plate please sir". Mr. Talbot was talking so I just took his plate and gave it to the servant. He turned round and said "Thank you ma'am", and afterwards I found out he had not finished. It was a capital joke at the time!'

When she married in 1854, her new husband's niece Lucy wrote in her own diary that Emily was 'charitable, young (21), amiable, humble, good-looking.' Lucy grew up to become Lady Lucy Cavendish, a pioneer of education for women, and her own diaries were published in 1927.

In Emily's own diary she recorded her education regime and wrote on August 26th 1844: 'At present I do French exercises for ¾ hour, Maps 1 hour, Music 1¼, read French and English, ¾ hour, write French copy ½ hour. I like doing Maps very much; they are traced out, and one only has to put the names in and paint it. I have made this description in case I get married and have children it may be useful to them.'

In the same entry for August 26th she admitted that 'I was looking in Mama's trunk for something the other day and the first thing I saw was, at the top of a great many Journal books or something of that sort a piece of paper on which was written "If I die, let these be burnt", and something else which I did not see! I am sure I should like to see them very much, and I do not see why they should be burnt.'

Alas, Emily did not have any children and died aged only forty-four. Her husband, thirteen years her senior, died seven years later and made provision in his will for the Lady Lucy Lyttleton Fund, to support nursing in the local community. Her childhood diary came into the possession of the Nutt family, who used its empty pages for shopping lists and, in the case of a certain Arthur Nutt, to write out repeatedly 'Arthur Nutt is a good boy. Good boys are happy.'

Eventually, the journal was rediscovered by a descendent of the Nutts, fourteen-year-old Dee Cooper, and published in 1984. We must be grateful that it wasn't destroyed in the intervening 140 years since Emily began to write it.

RIGHT: Emily's diary was recorded for just six months of her life. She went on to live until the age of forty-four.

Maria Heyde, German missionary in Tibet

(1837–1913)

'This afternoon I received the news that I am engaged to be married' wrote the Moravian missionary Wilhelm Heyde on May 11th 1859. The news was no less of a surprise to his bride Maria, whose diary of their life together in Tibet is a densely woven tapestry of interactions with many cultures.

Maria Hartmann was born in Paramaribo, the capital of Suriname, to German Moravian missionaries. She followed in her parents' footsteps and at the age of twenty-two she was asked by her church to travel to Tibet and become the wife of Wilhelm Heyde, who had already been in the region for eight years. Such arranged marriages were common practice in the Moravian Church and Hartmann herself was the product of one.

Trusting in her God she accepted the proposal and travelled, with two brides of Wilhelm's fellow missionaries, to the Indian subcontinent. She was the youngest, and the only one of the three who had not known her fiancé before her betrothal to him. In Calcutta Maria received her first contact with her husband-to-be, a letter in which he introduced himself. She was overwhelmed, and relieved. 'With what tender love you meet me!', she wrote in her diary on September 24th 1859. 'Ah! I am not worthy of it; if you knew my heart with its doubts, fears, and resistance, you would be frightened. But you will come to know this heart entirely, to cherish and to console it, with the aid of God.'

When they finally met, it was at the opposite ends of a precarious rope footbridge over a mountain torrent near Kyelang, the location of the mission house. Maria was terrified and froze; so, Wilhelm crossed to her side and carried her across. It was a symbolic and sincere moment of their commitment to each other.

Wilhelm and Maria remained in Tibet for the next forty-four years. They worked hard and in partnership. Although some missionaries found it hard to gain acceptance in a strongly Hindu area, Maria and Wilhelm were popular among Tibetans, who came to know them as Mama and Papa Heyde.

Among their many contributions to the community was the knitting school which Maria set up. Tibetans spun thread and wove their clothing, but knitting was unknown until Maria's introduction. At its height the school attracted some ninety students, and Maria approached it industriously writing on 'January 11th 1865. I had [wool for] new socks to give out to some boys for knitting; washed 2 pairs of gray stockings to test whether the wool would hold the dye. ... Very busy in the afternoon at the knitting school, taking on a new girl. Spent almost the whole evening checking and altering stockings. Very late to bed.' The next day, 'January 12th. Morning, as always, busy with cooking, cleaning, stockings etc. In the afternoon the girls knitted in the porch, all in all, Thank God, it felt better today; finished the first pair of socks.'

The school made socks and stockings which were sold in India, bringing income both to the mission and to individual knitters. Such was the impact of her work that today knitted socks are considered a part of Tibetan national dress. Maria's diary is available today in German, edited by Frank Seeliger; and extracts from it and the diaries of other Tibetan missionaries are included in *Fifty Years Among the Tibetans – the story of Wilhelm and Marie Heyde* written by their son Gerhard Heyde.

ABOVE: Maria Heyde, was born in the Dutch Guiana, which is now Suriname. Her parents were both missionaries and she followed in their footsteps.

ABOVE: Charlotte Forten's diaries have been published in multiple editions and record her life in the divided American society of the late nineteenth century.

Charlotte Forten, American abolitionist

(1837–1914)

Charlotte Forten, a free woman of colour growing up in Salem, began her journal when she was sixteen out of 'a wish to record the passing events of my life, which, even if quite unimportant to others, naturally possess great interest to myself.' In reality, the diary is an invaluable record to historians of the antebellum North of the USA.

Charlotte was born in Philadelphia. Her father came from a long line of abolitionists, but her mother was a freed slave, the result of a union between James Cathcart Johnston, a wealthy plantation owner, and Charlotte's enslaved grandmother. Johnston had freed Charlotte, her three sisters and her mother and set them up in Philadelphia in 1833.

Charlotte found work as a maid in a household in Salem, where at school she was the only Black student among 200. It was here that she began her diary, writing on only its second day, May 25th 1854: 'Did not intend to write this evening, but have just heard of something that is worth recording. Another fugitive from bondage has been arrested; a poor man, who for two short months has trod the soil and breathed the air of the "Old Bay State" [Massachusetts] was arrested like a criminal in the streets of her capital, and is now kept strictly guarded … to prevent a man, whom God has created in his own image, from regaining that freedom with which, he, in common with every human being, is endowed.' The captured man was Anthony Burns: his subsequent return to his enslaver in Virginia was condemned by Boston abolitionists who eventually bought his freedom.

Charlotte trained as a teacher and subsequently became the first African American to be hired to teach White children in a Salem public school. Ill health forced her return to Philadelphia, where she became an energetic anti-slavery activist. In 1859, history seemed to be repeating itself, as she noted on April 4th: 'Heard to-day that there has been another fugitive arrested. There is to be a trial. God grant that the poor man may be released from the clutches of the slavehunters.'

Only two days later however, 'Good news! After waiting with intense and painful anxiety for the result of the three days' trial we are at last gladdened by the news that the alleged fugitive, Daniel [Webster], has been released. … It is encouraging to know that there was so much right and just feeling about the matter. It gives one some hope even for Philadelphia.'

Four days after his first mention, on April 8th, a large meeting celebrated Daniel's release. 'A crowd of Southerners was present and ere the meeting had progressed far they created a great disturbance, stamping, hallooing, groaning etc. … At one time there was a precipitate rush forward. We thought we should be crushed, but I did not feel at all frightened; I was too excited to think of fear.'

Webster was still in danger of being arrested, and it was with relief that Charlotte was able to report on April 23rd, 'D[aniel] has left us and we hear with joy that he is safe in Canada. Oh, stars and stripes, that wave so proudly over our mockery of freedom, what is your protection.'

Walburga, Lady Paget, German occultist and friend of Queen Victoria

(1839-1929)

Lady Paget, wife of British diplomat Sir Augustus Paget, led a privileged life at the highest levels of European society. Her husband served as British Ambassador in Copenhagen, Vienna, Portugal, Florence and Rome and Lady Paget wrote it all down in her wry, waspish observations.

Walburga was born in 1839 in Berlin, the daughter of Count Karl Friedrich Anton von Hohenthal and his second wife, Countess Emilie Niedhart von Gneisenau. Before her marriage, Countess Walburga Ehrengarde Helena von Hohenthal was a lady-in-waiting to Queen Victoria's eldest child, Princess Victoria. She and Queen Victoria became close friends, to the extent that Sir Augustus and Lady Walburga named their first child Victor in her honour, and their second Alberta Victoria after the queen and her German husband Prince Albert of Saxe-Coburg and Gotha.

Walburga's diaries formed the basis for several volumes of her memoirs, and in the preface to one of them, *Embassies of Other Days*, she included a warning, 'I always see the faults of my friends. But I like their faults and I mention them as it adds to the piquancy of their personalities.'

Lady Paget was not a "tell-all auto-biographer", but her accounts are certainly revealing. At the conclusion of *Embassies of Other Days* she issued a half-hearted apology. 'I have related everything exactly as it appeared to me to be and may thereby have inadvertently hurt the feelings of some, but this must be put to the account of my sincerity.'

Lady Paget's sincerity was not always affectionate. Of Freiin Marie "Mary" von Vetsera, a Viennese socialite who disappeared under mysterious and scandalous circumstances, probably related to her infatuation with Rudolph, Crown Prince of the Habsburg Empire, Lady Paget wrote that she was a 'pretty but fast girl. I never liked her on account of her flirtations with married men'.

Walburga was closely involved in the arranged marriage of Queen Victoria's eldest son the Prince of Wales (and future King Edward VII) to Princess Alexandra of Denmark, while Sir Augustus Paget occupied his ambassadorial post in that country's capital, Copenhagen. Walburga, whom Victoria addressed as Wally, knew that the queen was searching for a suitable bride, and felt that she would have to look far and wide to find a better match for her son than the princess.

Lady Paget arranged a meeting between the queen and the princess, which took place in Brussels. 'Just before the meeting,' she noted, 'I was with the Queen in a small boudoir adjoining the room where the Danish and Belgian royalties were assembled. The Queen suddenly stood up and, resting her head on my shoulder, burst into tears and said: "You, dear Wally, will quite understand what I feel at this moment; you have a husband you love and you know what I have lost."' Her beloved Prince Albert had died in 1861, only a year earlier.

Victoria was delighted with her first impression of Princess Alexandra, and the deal was sealed with a grand banquet the next day, after which the Prince of Wales 'said to me, "Now I will take a walk with Princess Alix in the garden and in three quarters of an hour I will take her into the grotto and there I will propose and I hope it will be to everybody's satisfaction."'

'I was much amused,' Lady Paget added, 'at this practical way of mapping out the future, but I had noticed that the Prince, in the day or two which he had been together with the Princess, had become very much interested in her and alive to her beauty and charm.'

ABOVE: Lady Paget's accounts were faithful to the point they were almost scandalous. In her memoirs, she would reference people by name, even those who did not wish to be identified.

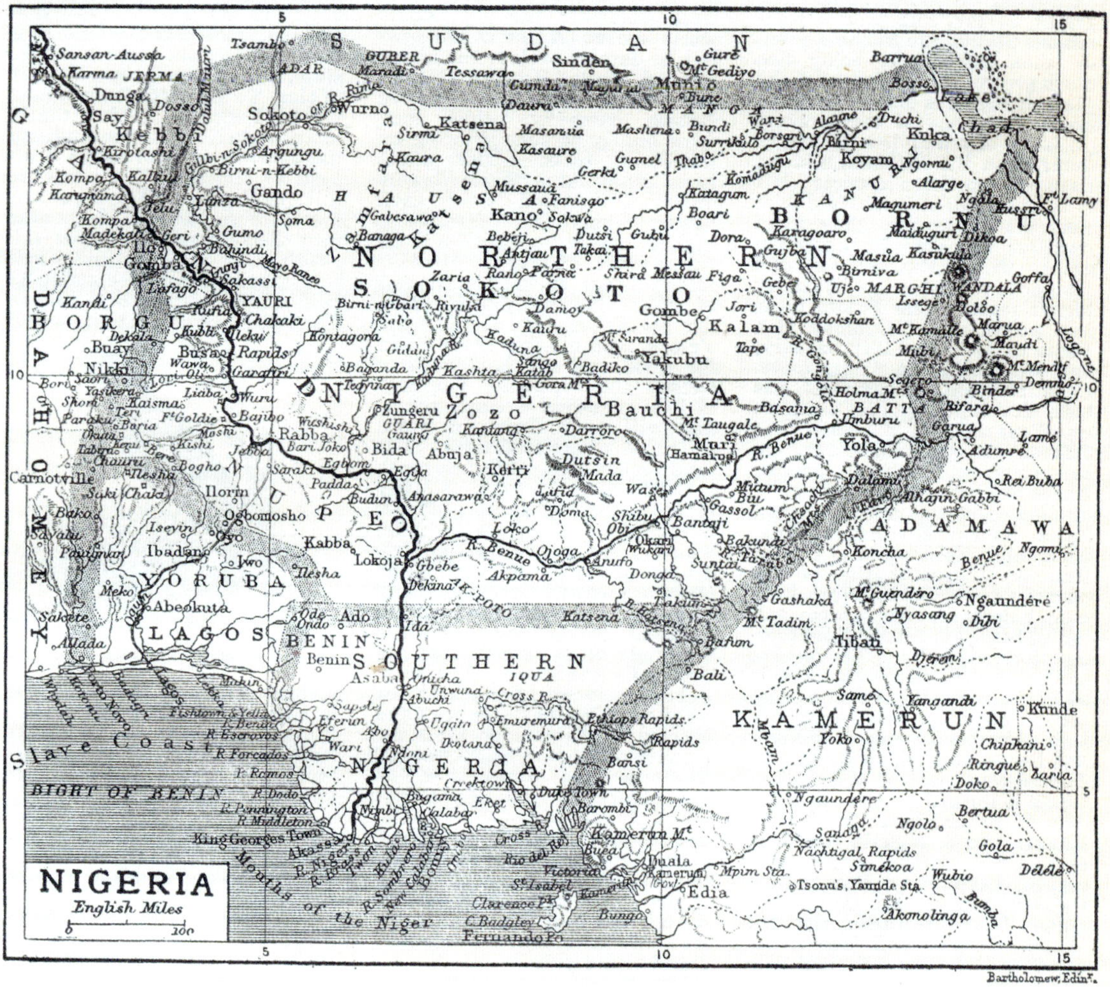

ABOVE: A historic map of Nigeria from the 1900s.
RIGHT: An aroko similar to the one sent to the UK by John Augustus.

John Augustus Otunba-Payne, Nigerian court registrar

(1839–1906)

John Otunba-Payne's *Lagos and West African Almanack and Diary* was an annual event in the Nigerian capital. Like a conventional almanac it contained useful local information, but was also an annual summary of Payne's personal journeys throughout the region in search of its history.

Born John Augustus Payne, he was descended from a royal family of the Ijebu kingdom. Payne's surname was a corruption of Adepeyin, and he adopted the additional surname Otunba, which means 'aide to the king' in Yoruba, the dominant language of the region. Payne was an early product of the Church Missionary Society Grammar School in Lagos, founded in 1859 and intended to educate local people for public service, not only within the Christian church but to increase the proportion of Nigerians working in the colonial administration of the time.

Payne rose to become Chief Registrar of the Supreme Court of Lagos and a prominent citizen of the city. He travelled widely to document the oral history of the region. Historians today owe him a large debt of gratitude for preserving information which would otherwise have been lost or distorted with the passage of time.

Payne's *Almanack and Diary*, published every year from 1873 to at least 1894, recorded military and diplomatic events, significant weddings and funerals (as is the traditional fare of local newspapers the world over), population information and trade statistics. It grew larger every year, expanded as the results of his latest journeys. His introduction to the 1886 edition refers to its scale, 'much enlarged beyond that of its predecessors, for a considerable number of Articles are added each year – such as Remarkable Occurrences, Table of Ordnances, Slave Trade Suppression Tables,' – and a new item of which he was exceptionally proud – 'Native African Mode of Communication (called Aroko – ie hieroglyphic or African Symbolical Letters).'

This last was an illustrated report on a remarkable method of sending messages in a culture with no alphabet and no written records, which may already have been dying out when Payne wrote it. What might appear to the ignorant eye as a number of superstitious charms made of cowrie shells, twigs and feathers were actually letters from one Ijebu to another, in which the arrangements of their elements could be understood symbolically.

For example, Payne wrote, six cowries threaded onto a feather which is then bent back alongside the shells meant, 'By these six cowries I draw you to myself and you should also draw closely to me. As by this feather I can only reach to your ears, so I am expecting [or asking] you to come to me, or hoping to see you immediately.'

As Payne explained, the word for the number six was derived from the verb "to draw"; and by tradition a feather was the only tool considered clean enough to be used in the inner ear. The understanding of symbols implied a capacity for metaphor, and therefore for poetry, of which western minds had not imagined the heathen Africans capable. Payne wanted the wider world to know about his culture, and sent the items themselves to the Royal Anthropological Society of Great Britain and Ireland, where a talk on them was given the same year. Unfortunately for Payne, they did not precipitate the academic interest which he had hoped for and they now languish in the Pitt Rivers Museum in Oxford.

Pyotr Ilyich Tchaikovsky, Russian composer

(1840–1893)

Tchaikovsky was a sporadic diarist, too busy writing music to be conscientious about a daily journal. He did however make several valiant attempts to renew his habit and a large body of his personal thoughts survives to shine a light on the mind of this great romantic composer.

Tchaikovsky's first diary entry of 1886 was not written until February 13th. This entry is typical of his writing style, a jumble of incomplete thoughts and impulses which he seemed in a hurry to get down on paper. 'Shall I ever finish this diary?,' he wailed. 'God alone knows! I should very much like to finish it and start many more. How much there is still to do! How much to read! How much to learn! I so terribly don't want to die yet, although sometimes it seems that I've lived for such a long time on this world. The weather was good but overcast.' Few composers take up music to become rich; and on the same day he bemoaned the fact that 'Alyosha [his loyal servant] brought no post, and I'm impatiently awaiting a letter with an enclosure—I have no money at all.'

Tchaikovsky, the composer of theatrical masterpieces such as *Swan Lake, The Nutcracker* and *Eugene Onegin* and eternally popular classics like the *Romeo and Juliet Overture* and his *Piano Concerto No. 1*, had his demons. He regularly burned sections of diaries in which he later regretted what he had confessed to or had agonised over; and as such there are no surviving references to his homosexuality. His excessive drinking however is frequently recorded, with regret. On July 11th 1886 Tchaikovsky contemplated it wryly. 'It is said that to abuse oneself with alcoholic drink is harmful,' he acknowledged. 'I readily agree with that. But nevertheless, I, a sick person, full of neuroses, absolutely cannot do without the poison against which Mr Miklukho-Maklai [a prominent Russian anthropologist] protests. A person with such a strange name is extremely happy that he does not know the delights of vodka and other alcoholic drinks. But how unjust it is to judge others by yourself and to prohibit to others that which you yourself do nor like. Now I, for example. am drunk every night, and cannot do without it. What should I do then?'

Two days later however the composer recalled one of the happiest moments in his life to date, his meeting with the Russian novelist Leo Tolstoy. Tchaikovsky feared that Tolstoy, the great observer of the human condition, would trigger and probe all the composer's deepest insecurities. 'I was overcome by fear and a sense of awkwardness in front of him. It seemed to me that this supreme student of human nature would, with one glance, be able to penetrate into all the recesses of my soul. In his presence, so I thought, there was no longer any way of successfully concealing all the rubbish which I have at the bottom of my soul.' In fact, Tolstoy proved to be 'a simple, sound, and sincere person' and even perhaps a little narrow-minded, in Tchaikovsky's opinion, in his dislike of the music of Beethoven.

When it came to the music of Tchaikovsky however, 'perhaps never in my life has my composer's pride been so flattered and moved as when L N Tolstoy, sitting beside me and listening to the Andante from my First Quartet, burst into tears.'

ABOVE: Tchaikovsky is perhaps most famous for his ballets: Swan Lake *(1877),* The Sleeping Beauty *(1889) and* The Nutcracker *(1892).*

ABOVE: Treloar a year before his death. Throughout his life he wore many hats: businessman, Sheriff of London, and eventually Lord Mayor of London.

LEFT: An original advertisement by Treloar and Sons, from 13th June 1887.

William Purdie Treloar, English haberdasher and Lord Mayor of London

(1843–1923)

A Londoner born and bred, William Treloar began work as a travelling salesman for his father's business selling coconut fibre mats, carpets and Turkish rugs. It must have been his regular contact with the public which spurred Treloar's interest in local politics, in which he later rose to the highest level.

Treloar's business prospered and in time the company had premises facing each other on either side of Ludgate Hill, which a fanciful advertisement for the company made the most of by depicting a Wilton carpet running the length of the street between them.

Treloar entered politics in 1881, first as a councillor then as alderman for the ward of Farrington Without. The death in 1898 of his brother, Robert, who had been increasingly responsible for the running of the stores, brought about the closure of the family firm, and the following year William became a Sherriff of the City of London. The pinnacle of his political career was his appointment, in 1906, as the Lord Mayor of London.

Unlike the office of "mere" Mayor of London which manages the budget and services of the city, the Lord Mayor has a largely ceremonial role, within which they are responsible for promoting the businesses of the city of London. The Lord Mayor hosts banquets at which senior politicians make speeches, attends openings, and raises funds for their chosen charitable cause.

Treloar kept a diary of his year in office, which he published in 1920. It was an eventful twelve months, November to November. Two future branches of the London Underground system opened, including, on November 15th 1906, the Piccadilly Line. For Treloar, it was a typical day: 'Attended the opening of the Piccadilly and Brompton Railway, now known as the Piccadilly Tube; and Sir E. Speyer afterwards presided at a luncheon at the Criterion Restaurant. Mr. Lloyd George was presented with a silver key as a memento of the occasion.' Future Prime Minister Lloyd George was President of the Board of Trade at the time. Sir Edgar Speyer was the head of the predecessor of the London Underground, the Underground Electric Railways Company of London.

London introduced fare meters for taxicabs on March 22nd 1907; but Treloar's thoughts were elsewhere. His choice of charity for the year was what he called a Cripples Fund, with the aim of building a hospital away from the polluted air of the city for children with non-pulmonary tuberculosis. Over the course of his year in office Treloar raised £10,000 for the project, and on the day that taximeters first appeared he drove out to Alton in Hampshire, where a site had been found.

He describes the event,'went to Alton by motorcar. My first visit. A memorable occasion. There had been erected at Alton, on seventy acres of sloping grassland, bungalows to serve as a hospital for soldiers wounded in the South African War. With the passing of time, the need and usefulness of these buildings had ceased and they were resting empty and tending to decay. Here was an opportunity. With the assistance of Lord Haldane, then Minister of State for War, those buildings and the freehold land on which they were erected became mine by Act of Parliament.'

Treloar's College opened in 1908 and still operates today, from a number of centres. The incumbent Lord Mayor, as part of their duties, still makes an annual visit to the original site in Alton.

Sofia Tolstaya, Russian diarist

(1844–1919)

It is good to be able to see both sides of an argument, and what a long argument there was in the Tolstoy household. Both Leo and Sofia Tolstoy kept diaries throughout the forty-seven miserable years of their unhappy marriage, one of the most notoriously ill-matched unions in literary history.

Tolstoy's novel *Anna Karenina* opens with the pertinent observation that 'all happy families are alike, but each unhappy family is unhappy in its own way'. Leo Tolstoy was sixteen years older than Sofia, and they first met when she was a child and he was a friend of her mother's. His marriage proposal was made not in a romantic moonlit setting but by post. Leo was already a successful novelist and she, who had looked up to him since she was a young girl, accepted his invitation readily.

The pair were married only a week later, but not before he had taken the extraordinary step, on the eve of the wedding, of giving her a list of all his former lovers. Sofia was horrified to discover that she was not his first and only love. Even worse, one of the women on the list was a servant still working on the family estate which was about to become her home, and with whom Leo had fathered a child.

'The whole of my husband's past is so ghastly that I don't think I shall ever be able to accept it,' she wrote in her diary. 'When he kisses me, I am always thinking, "I am not the first woman he has loved". It hurts me so much that my love for him – the dearest thing in the world to me ... should not be enough for him.'

Married life was not full of the peace and comfortability as the young woman had dreamt of, and after only a year Tolstaya had begun to realise that 'I am to gratify his pleasure and nurse his child, I am a piece of household furniture, I am a woman. I try to suppress all human feelings. When the machine is working properly it heats the [breast] milk and bustles about trying not to think – and life is tolerable.'

Tolstoy refused to practice contraception, and Sofia endured no fewer than sixteen pregnancies. Three ended in miscarriages; three more died within a year of their birth; and two others died before their eighth birthdays. Tolstoy's lust was one thing, but during pregnancy he lost all interest in her. 'My pregnancy is to blame for everything,' she noted bitterly. 'I'm in an unbearable state, physically and mentally. As far as Lyova [an affectionate version of the name Leo] is concerned I don't exist.'

As Tolstoy's success increased, she found herself juggling not only her maternal duties but the management of the estate, and of her husband's busy career. She handled his financial affairs, dealt with correspondence, appointments, copyright and state censorship and – in an age before photocopiers and computers – wrote out fair copies of his latest works by hand. Tolstoy's epic masterpiece *War and Peace* is a challenging novel to read just once; Sofia had to write it out seven times, by candlelight late at night after she had finished all her other chores, from her husband's almost illegible handwritten notes.

ABOVE: Sofia Tolstaya was the long-suffering wife of writer Leo Tolstoy, most famous for his book War and Peace.

ABOVE: Alice hailed from an illustrious family: one brother, Henry James, was a novelist; and another, William James, was a psychologist and philosopher.

Alice James, American diarist and sister of novelist Henry James

(1848-1892)

Alice James suffered all her life from a persistent and debilitating neurological condition which was either ignored or misdiagnosed as hysteria by a medical profession which still believed, as her doctor did, that 'women are emotional as a class of human beings'. Her diary displays astonishing cheerfulness and resilience.

Alice's physician Dr Charles Fayette Taylor blamed Alice's delicate constitution on an excess of education. Education was acceptable in her over-achieving brothers, author Henry and psychologist William, but 'for patience, for reliability ... for self-control, give me the little woman who has not been "educated" too much, and whose only ambition is to be a wife and mother.' For her part, Alice retorted, in the privacy of her diary, that 'one has a greater sense of degradation after an interview with a doctor than from any human experience.'

Alice was fully the intellectual and creative equal of her brothers, capable of the psychological insights of William and the linguistic brilliance of Henry. She first realised its potential for her when, during one long, dull visit to some family friends when they were children, Henry turned quietly to her and commented subversively, 'well, this is a kind of fun, one could say.' She laughed uncontrollably, and the remark opened up an entire world of irony, deprecation, and coded truth. Years later Alice saw in that moment the start of her inner life, and her diary is full of sharp wit.

Her pain drove her to distraction, and she often contemplated suicide or patricide – her father had little to offer her in the way of comfort besides urging her to be brave, to be good, to be happy. 'How sick one gets of being good,' she wrote. 'How heroic to be able to suppress one's vanity to the extent of confessing that the game is too hard. Ah, those strange people who have the courage to be unhappy!'

Alice's mind was too active for her to lead a passive life as society dictated women should lead. Toward the end of her teenage years, 'when I broke down first, acutely, and had violent turns of hysteria, ... I saw so distinctly that it was a fight simply between my body and my will, a battle in which the former was to be triumphant to the end.' With this realisation she made a decision – to abandon her body to its fate in order to preserve her mind – to lose what she described as her 'muscular sanity' in favour of her mental stability.

In later years she described the process: 'So, with the rest, you abandon the pit of your stomach, the palms of your hands, the soles of your feet, and refuse to keep them sane when you find in turn one moral impression after another producing despair in the one, terror in the others, anxiety in the third and so on until life becomes one long flight from remote suggestion and complicated eluding of the multifold traps set for your undoing.'

Alice James' diary is an uplifting read, affirming her positive mental sanity till the end – which came not from madness or hysteria, but from breast cancer, when she was only forty-three. She dictated her last diary entry to her lifelong companion Katharine Loring, as she felt herself slipping finally away. 'Physical pain however great ends in itself and falls away like dry husks from the mind. ... I go no longer in dread. Oh the wonderful moment when I felt myself floated for the first time into the deep sea of divine cessation, and saw all the dear old mysteries and miracles vanish into vapour!'

Tomas O'Crohan, Irish islander

(1856–1937)

It is no small irony that Tomas O'Crohan, a native Irish speaker on Great Blasket Island, was taught to read and write English by a Yorkshireman from London's British Museum who had come to the island to learn Irish. With his new skills at his disposal, he set about recording daily island life.

Great Blasket Island lies about 2km off of the Dingle Peninsula in western Ireland. In the nineteenth century its population of around 150 lived a simple subsistence life: catching fish which they sold on the mainland, where they could buy life's little luxuries such as soap, flour, tobacco and paraffin – the only source of heat and light apart from peat. Apart from fish, the residents, diet consisted of potatoes, wild rabbits, seabirds and their eggs, and one of Thomas's ten children died in a fall from a cliff while trying to catch a fledgling gull.

Relatively remote from the rest of the country, the islanders spoke some of the purest Irish Gaelic in the land, despite the ban on the language imposed by English settlers at several times in its history. It was in pursuit of this pure form that the Yorkshireman Robin Flower came to the island. He and Tomas became firm friends and when Tomas wrote a history of the island, it was Robin who translated it into English.

Tomas O'Crohan's diary is a simple report of the events and conversations of the day. He gives a plain, unadorned account of Blasket life and its attraction is in Tomas's instinctive skill as a storyteller. The stories are more or less trivial but told with charm and dry humour. A typical entry from May 1919, recalls a meeting with some young women collecting limpets.

'What implements do you have for scraping them off?' Tomas remembers asking them. "I have the broken half of a pair of shears. The other girl has an iron bolt, but the limpets aren't too plentiful here."

'Why didn't ye send yeer mothers to gather them? Wouldn't they have more skill and craft for the work?

"But how would we ever learn if they always came to gather them?" said she.

"Holy Mary! Isn't it grand to be here by the sea's edge at low tide! The lovely smell that's there when everything that was under the sea before is under the sun now and its mouth gaping. I dare say the people of Dublin would love to be here at this time."'

It was not always easy to live on Blasket. Storms could isolate the island for weeks at a time. Once a huge catch of fish had to be thrown back into the sea because the ruthless mainland fish merchants offered too little for it to be worthwhile landing the catch – and without a decent price the fishermen could not afford the salt to preserve the fish themselves. 'Not many kind words were said about the merchants of Dingle,' Tomas noted with understatement.

Tomas O'Crohan's diary was published in 1928, in a translation which manages to retain the rhythm of the Irish language without anglicising it. O'Crohan's diary unleashed a flood of other publications by Blasket authors which revealed the island to have an unrivalled talent for storytelling. Alas, the way of life which they recorded could not last forever. Industrial trawling depleted the seas, while poverty, hardship and the lure of modern life on the mainland depleted the population. The Irish State declared the island unviable and removed the last of its inhabitants in 1954. Tomas O'Crohan's house now serves as a tourist attraction.

ABOVE: *Tomas O'Crohan would perhaps be heartened to know his language survives today. The 2022 census recorded almost 2 million people as able to speak Irish in Ireland and Northern Ireland.*

ABOVE: A photograph of Ida in the early twentieth century. Eight years after her marriage, in 1890, the Church of Latter-Day Saints formally renounced polygamy, with the policy formalised in 1905.

Ida Hunt Udall, American homesteader

(1858–1915)

Ida Hunt Udall's conversion to the idea of polygamy, and her experience of it as her husband's second wife, were recorded in her diary for four tumultuous years. A devout Mormon, Ida Hunt Udall experienced love and disappointment within her chosen lifestyle, and hostility from outside of it.

During the nineteenth century, the Church of Latter-day Saints, also known as Mormons, believed that plural marriage – in which one man would take more than one wife – was a religious practice. This polygamy was widely abhorred by those outside of the Mormon Church, whether through a lack of understanding, jealousy, or a different interpretation of Christianity.

Mormon polygamy was not universal: those choosing it accounted for between 20 and 64 per cent of the church's congregation. A federal Act had outlawed the practice in 1862 and was reinforced by another act banning co-habitation outside marriage in 1882, only two months before Ida's marriage to David Udall. Ida was forced into hiding for the next four years, and rarely cohabited with David and his first wife Ella thereafter. In 1890 the president of the Latter-day Saints, Wilford Woodruff, ended the church's sanction of polygamy, advising all Mormons to obey Federal Law.

Ida Hunt was born into a monogamous Mormon family which moved frequently around the west and mid-west of the United States. During one journey, accompanying a polygamous family, she was moved by the spirituality of the arrangement and decided that she wanted to be a plural wife. Soon afterwards she rejected a proposal from her then-boyfriend who insisted on monogamy.

David Udall was the owner of a general store in which she worked as a clerk. He and Ella had just had their first child, and he began to court Ida in 1881. Ella was the daughter of polygamous Mormon parents; but while she agreed with polygamy in theory, she was less happy with the prospect of it in reality. She and Ida exchanged letters on the subject and Ella wrote that 'if it is the Lord's will I am perfectly willing to try to endure it.' It was hardly a ringing endorsement and Ella's antipathy, as well as her status as first wife, blighted Ida's role in the family for the rest of their time together.

On the wedding night however, all was smiles. Ida wrote in her journal, 'When he bade me goodnight, the sacred name of wife was whispered for the first time in my ear, causing my heart to flutter with a strange new happiness. During the night, Ella, being unable to sleep, came into my room, and mentioned for the first time our relationship to each other, and we talked long and earnestly of our hopes and desires for the future, both feeling much happier for the same.'

Soon afterwards, Ida began to be aware of hostility towards her and other polygamous Mormons. Her local newspaper, the *Apache Chief*, published a feature calling for the lynching of her father, her husband and her husband's father. She too was named and shamed; and she complained in her diary that the paper's 'sole mission was to misrepresent and vilify our people. ... My name frequently come out in glowing colors, calling me a prostitute, mistress etc. This was very hard for our brethren to bear, but they treated it with silent contempt, and quit reading the paper altogether.'

David was tried for polygamy and convicted of perjury although eventually pardoned by US President Grover Cleveland. Ida's diary ends with his release and the dropping of the perjury charges in 1886.

Sir Roger Casement, Irish Nationalist

(1864-1916)

Fictional diaries and forgeries are beyond the scope of the present book, but the diaries of British diplomat Roger Casement, circulated by the British government in an attempt to discredit him and once thought to be faked, are now accepted by most observers as genuine.

Casement, a once loyal and trusted civil servant, was hung for treason in 1916 for his involvement in Ireland's Easter Rising. Before he came to support the Irish cause, he served as a British consul in the Congo, Portugal and Brazil. He was admired for exposing the systematic abuse of the Congolese population by the King of Belgium. In Peru, where he investigated the casual disregard for human life shown by a Portuguese rubber-harvesting company towards the enslaved Putamayo Indian people, he wrote that 'it far exceeds in depravity and demoralisation the Congo regime at its worst.'

It was precisely these acts of colonial cruelty which began to turn Casement against imperialism. He was born in Dublin, an Anglo-Irishman – a descendant of English and Scottish settlers who were planted in Ireland to exercise British control over the country. Casement saw similarities between Britain's suppression of Irish language, culture and self-determination and the European abuse of indigenous populations across Africa and South America.

Irish activists saw an opportunity for an uprising in 1916 while Britain was distracted by the greater conflict in Europe. Casement negotiated with Britain's enemy, Germany for political support, and for a shipment of German guns – which were intercepted by the British Navy before they reached Ireland. He was subsequently tried for treason and sentenced to death. His admirers appealed for clemency and to quieten their voices the British Government circulated extracts from his diary, which contained detailed accounts of his homosexuality – still illegal in Britain at the time. The revelations had the desired effect, and he was duly hanged.

Casement's supporters became convinced that the diaries were faked by the British Secret Service. Doubts about their validity persisted for the rest of the century. Historians and hand-writing experts however are convinced that they are genuine. They contain details of names and places in his public and private life that only he and a very few others could have known.

The situation is complicated by the fact that Roger Casement kept not one but two sets of diaries. One recorded the everyday activities of his political and diplomatic life; the other contained the much more personal material on which the British Government pounced. Compare these two entries for the same day, December 10th 1910.

The first is from the so-called White Diaries: 'Out for a walk to the military firing ground with Ignacio Torres as my guide. Took several photos of the ground and trees and a stream beyond. Back at 11 - in great heat - and wrote a little in the afternoon altho' it was stifling. In the evening the Cazes' had a bridge party after dinner which lasted till midnight - and the heat lasted all night. It was really atrocious - not a breath of air and I lay for hours trying to sleep - and then got up and wrote, but the mosquitoes stop that game.'

The second from the Black Diaries - 'Sunday. 4th DEC. Very hot morning. Looking out window saw Ignacio waiting. Joy. Off with him to Tirotero and Camera. Bathed & photo'd & talked & back at 11. Gave 4/-. At 5.30 Cajamarca policeman till 7 at Bella Vista & again at 10.30 passeando & at 8 long talk. Shook hands and offered. Tall, Inca type & brown. Cards & Bridge & stupid party till near midnight. Saw Cajamarca several times from window.'

ABOVE: A portrait of Robert Casement, who was executed by the United Kingdom for treason in 1916.

ABOVE : A photograph of Marie and her husband Pierre Curie, in 1895. The pair were the first married couple to win the Nobel Prize in its history.

Marie Curie, Polish physicist and chemist

(1867–1934)

Marie Curie's achievements, not only for science but for women in science, were remarkable: she was the first woman to win a Nobel Prize, the first person to win two Nobel Prizes, and the only one to win them in different disciplines. Her diaries show her commitment to the laboratory, and the comfort she found there.

Curie won her first Nobel in 1903, for Physics, sharing it with her husband Pierre Curie and the French physicist Henri Becquerel, for the discovery of radioactivity – a word which she invented. Her second came in 1911, for Chemistry, for her discovery of the radioactive elements radium and polonium.

Polonium was named after the country of her birth, Poland. She had moved from Warsaw to Paris in 1891 to further her studies. It was there she met Pierre in 1894; he had found a space in his laboratory for her to conduct research. The couple were married within a year, finding in each other a companion in life and science.

Their wedding was not religious, and instead of a bridal gown Marie wore a dark blue suit which was then pressed into service as laboratory wear. Marie and Pierre were too busy with their work to attend the Nobel ceremony in Stockholm, and only found time to collect their prize two years later. Tragedy struck in April 1906 however, when Pierre was killed in a traffic accident in Paris.

Pierre had given up his own research to work on his wife's; and the University of Paris had at last agreed to fund the laboratory, which they badly needed if they were to make further progress. Yet now he was gone. On the day he was placed in his coffin, Marie described in her diary how she placed beside him 'the little picture of me that you called "the good little student" and that you loved, ... the picture of her who had the happiness of pleasing you enough so that you did not hesitate to offer to share your life with her. ... You often told me that this was the only occasion in your life when you acted without hesitation, with the absolute conviction that you were doing well. My Pierre, I think you were not wrong. We were made to live together, and our union had to be.'

Over the weeks that followed, she used her diary to perpetuate his presence as long as she could, writing her thoughts directly to him. 'My little Pierre,' she began on May 14th, 'I want to tell you that the laburnum is in flower, the wisteria, the hawthorn and the iris are beginning—you would have loved all that. ... I want to tell you that I no longer love the sun or the flowers. The sight of them makes me suffer. I feel better on dark days like the day of your death, and if I have not learned to hate fine weather it is because my children have need of it.'

Marie threw herself into her work. 'I cannot conceive of anything which would give me real personal happiness,' she wrote, 'except perhaps scientific work, and not even that, because, if successful, I would be distressed that you didn't know about it. This laboratory gives me an illusion of preserving the remains of your life.' And even there, there were painful reminders of past happiness. 'I found a little picture of you near the scales, with such a lovely smiling expression that I can't look at it without sobbing, since I will never again see that sweet smile.'

Pierre and Marie were both buried in lead-lined coffins, and her diaries and notebooks are still stored in lead, because of the high levels of radiation to which they exposed themselves during their lives.

Robert Falcon Scott, English Antarctic explorer

(1868–1912)

Scott of the Antarctic, as he is heroically known, was a British naval officer who spent the last twelve years of his life exploring the Antarctic continent. The diary of his last expedition contains, in the face of imminent death, some of the most quintessentially British expressions of the "stiff upper lip".

Robert Falcon Scott was thirteen years old when he began his naval career as a sea cadet on England's south coast. He served on several ships as a junior officer before bumping into an old acquaintance on a street in London. The man, Clement Markham, president of the Royal Geographical Society, was mounting an expedition to explore the Antarctic. Scott quickly volunteered to lead it, and the expedition finally set sail in *HMS Discovery* in 1901.

The members of the expedition were woefully inexperienced in polar conditions, but this first visit to the continent, from 1901 to 1903, made valuable scientific discoveries and delivered important experience for all involved. Scott had originally offered to lead it because of the rise in pay and status it would afford – his father and brother had both died recently, leaving him the main breadwinner of his family. But in those two years the Antarctic worked its magic on him and in 1906 he proposed a second expedition, this time with the aim of reaching the South Pole itself.

Scott's ship the *Terra Nova* set sail in the northern summer of 1910, with the intention of arriving during the early summer of the southern hemisphere. On the way he learned that the Norwegian explorer Roald Amundsen was also making a bid for the pole. After trials of their various forms of transport – caterpillar trucks, horses, dogs and manpower – they were ready to set off in November 1911, the Antarctic Spring. But at the end of the first month the limitations of the Mongolian horses they had brought were beginning to show. 'The surface was much worse to-day,' Scott noted, 'the ponies sinking to their knees very often. ... The dogs [from Siberia] are reported as doing very well. They are going to be a great standby, no doubt.'

Six weeks later, the expedition made a crushing discovery. 'We marched on,' Scott wrote on January 16th 1912, 'found ... a black flag tied to a sledge bearer; near by the remains of a camp; sledge tracks and ski tracks going and coming and the clear trace of dogs' paws – many dogs. This told us the whole story. The Norwegians have forestalled us and are first at the Pole. It is a terrible disappointment. ... All the day dreams must go; it will be a wearisome return.' Reaching the South Pole, Scott found a tent containing a letter from Amundsen.

With morale at its lowest the return journey was painfully slow. Lawrence Oates suffered terribly from frost bite, and on March 17th Scott recorded that '[Oates] slept through the night before last, hoping not to wake; but he woke in the morning – yesterday. It was blowing a blizzard. He said, "I am just going outside and may be some time." He went out into the blizzard and we have not seen him since.'

With supplies exhausted, and finding themselves trapped in their tent throughout a nine-day blizzard, Scott's final diary entry, on March 29th, was this:

'I do not think we can hope for any better things now. We shall stick it out to the end, but we are getting weaker, of course, and the end cannot be far. It seems a pity, but I do not think I can write more. R. SCOTT. For God's sake look after our people.'

RIGHT: A photograph of Robert Falcon Scott, or "Scott of the Antarctic" as he was sensationally portrayed in the 1948 film of the same name.

R.F. Scott
Captain R.N.

ABOVE : A 1920s photograph of Aleister. Educated at the University of Cambridge and a polarising figure to his contemporaries, he has been the subject of poetry, novels and song.

Aleister Crowley, English occultist and poet

(1875–1947)

Aleister Crowley is a hard man to define – libertine? prophet? devil? magician? monomaniac? His lifestyle was emotive fodder to the sensationalist press and it is difficult to see beyond the popular image of him as a lusty drug-taking satanist who inspired low-budget horror movies and paperback novels.

At his best Crowley was a seeker of universal truths, and he studied the religions, superstitions and rituals of other cultures in search of them. All those ideas coalesced in his own religion, Thelema, whose practice he summed up in this slogan: 'Do what thou wilt shall be the whole of the Law.' Crowley was a prolific author; of poetry, of the pseudo-biblical *The Book of the Law* on which Thelema was based, and even of occult fiction such as his novel *The Diary of a Drug Fiend*.

Drugs and sex played a central part in the occult initiation ceremonies which he devised and practiced; and Crowley encouraged his acolytes and initiates to keep diaries of their progress through the world of Magick which they invoked. He chose the archaic spelling of the word to differentiate his "real" magic from that of a stage magician.

Crowley regularly published his own diaries as guides for his followers, and they often recorded distinct periods of his life. He founded the Abbey of Thelema in 1920 as a centre for spiritual and temporal development, choosing the Villa Santa Barbara in Cefalù in Sicily as the location. It was not a success. Crowley himself had become addicted to heroin – he wrote *Diary of a Drug Fiend* during this period – and without any basic administrative management in place the Abbey descended into unsanitary chaos. After one young Thelemite died from drinking polluted water, his wife took the story to the British papers. The attention which this brought to the commune persuaded the Italian police to evict Crowley.

Crowley then moved to Tunisia and began a new diary, which has been published as *The Magical Diaries of Aleister Crowley: Tunisia 1923*. Much of it concerns the development of his esoteric ideas, with references which are impenetrable to the uninitiated, but there are more mundane matters discussed as well. In the first entry, on May 12th, he naturally finds time to rail against Italy. 'The newspaper this morning reported a serious affair at Messina,' he notes, 'where Mussolini's brigands made a murderous onslaught upon a peaceful political meeting. It is the beginning of the end for this upstart renegade with his gang of lawless ruffians and his crazy attempt to restore the tyranny of the Dark Ages. Only twenty-eight days since he signed the order for my expulsion from Italy, and already he totters.' If Crowley imagined that his expulsion would bring about the magical fall of Mussolini, it was a very slow magic: the Italian dictator rose to supreme power and was only toppled in the final year of World War Two.

The same diary page contains Crowley's prediction of the war. 'I divine a Jesuit conspiracy directed mainly against France; the idea is to get England and Germany to join it. A Catholic monarchy in Bavaria is doubtless an early item on this programme. I rather expect a war ... before the end of August this year. I hope that the USA will back France and keep England from plunging headlong to her final ruin.' War would indeed come, fourteen years later; and there were those who wished England to back Germany. Crowley concludes his thoughts with a literary plea: 'Oh England, England, will you not stand for the spirits of Milton, Shelley, Swinburne – and Aleister Crowley?'

Adam Czerniaków, Polish head of the Warsaw Ghetto's *Judenrat*

(1880–1942)

Only a few days after Warsaw surrendered to the invading forces of Nazi Germany in 1939, the city's Jewish population was corralled in the infamous Warsaw Ghetto. Adam Czerniaków was ordered to lead the Judenrat, the Jewish Council responsible for administering Nazi policy.

The position of leader was a poisoned chalice. Czerniaków risked being seen as a German henchman; and his scope for improving the lot of the doomed community was narrow indeed – he could wring only small concessions here and there from an otherwise increasingly brutal regime. On the one hand, Czerniaków had to maintain friendly relations with the German officers with whom he had to negotiate for even the smallest of victories; on the other, he wanted to keep morale up amidst increasingly alarming rumours of the fate of the Warsaw Jews. 'I am trying not to let the smile leave my face,' he wrote of his dealings with both the German and Jewish communities.

Czerniaków kept a secret diary of daily events from the arrival of the Germans until the start of the final deportations. It is written in a calm, matter-of-fact style, almost conversational in tone. The risk of discovery meant that Czerniaków could not risk making critical comments, or indeed remarks which might endanger the life of any Jewish people. He merely reported negotiations and outcomes; and this diary can be seen as a factual record for future historians to uncover what went on, as well as evidence of his own efforts to ameliorate the situation lest he be charged as a collaborator.

On July 17th 1942, for example, 'At 7 o'clock in the morning, a list of condemned prisoners, etc., was brought to my apartment for discussions with Schmied. ... Two Germans came at 11 A.M. and offered a barter transaction: if we supply shoes, etc., we will be permitted to purchase rye flour and some prisoners will be released.'

Two days later, rumours began to circulate: 'there is talk of about 40 railroad cars ready and waiting.' Despite German denials, panic rose in the Jewish community, and Czerniaków began to fear for the children, many of them orphaned. His wife worked at a children's home in the ghetto. 'Today I discussed with the Kommissar the problem of children in the detention center,' he wrote on July 20th. 'I talked this over with ... the manager of a transit center on Dzika Street. Some of the children would be placed there. ... It appears that about 2,000 children will qualify for reformatories.'

This was a lie. On July 22nd, 'Children were moved from the playground opposite the Community building. We were told that all the Jews irrespective of sex and age, with certain exceptions, will be deported to the East. By 4 P.M. today a contingent of 6,000 people must be provided. And this (at the minimum) will be the daily quota.' He was told to take up the matter of orphaned children with Sturmbannführer Höfle, the officer in charge of deportation. But Höfle had already told Czerniaków that 'if the deportation were impeded in any way, she would be the first one to be shot as a hostage.'

His final diary entry is dated July 23rd 1942. 'The orders are that there must be 9,000 by 4 o'clock,' he wrote at 3pm. His attempts to save the orphans had failed. Before taking a dose of cyanide which he had prepared the day the Germans first arrived in Warsaw, Adam Czerniaków wrote a note to his wife: 'They demand me to kill children of my nation with my own hands. I have nothing to do but to die.'

ABOVE : Adam Czerniaków first worked as a teacher in Warsaw. For many a symbol of resistance, he is now buried beside his wife at the Okopowa Street Jewish Cemetery in Warsaw, Poland.

Virginia Woolf, English author

(1882–1941)

Virginia Woolf's diary life encompassed two world wars. She began writing her first diary in earnest in 1915; and her last entry was in 1941, just four days before her death. The twenty-six volumes that Woolf left show just what a valuable writer's tool the act of journalling can be.

The act of writing was as essential to Virginia Woolf as the act of breathing and her journals fulfilled many functions for her. She wrote quickly, and often disjointedly, as if she had an urgent need to empty her mind onto the page. What arrived there might be her thoughts on the big news of the day, or her small encounters with friends and enemies. It might be the outpourings of the depressive thoughts which dogged her throughout her life, but she could just as easily switch suddenly to observations about the beauty of the world around her. 'I meant to write about death,' she wrote three weeks after her fortieth birthday, 'only life came breaking in as usual.' Writing down the dark thoughts was a way of purging them from her mind, at least for a while.

Woolf often described her diary entries as records of her life for her future self, and as an aid to writing an autobiography. Even before she reached the dreaded old age of fifty, she reread her diaries annually with a mixture of pleasure and surprise. 'If Virginia Woolf at the age of 50,' she wrote at the age of thirty-seven, 'when she sits down to build her memoirs out of these books, is unable to make a phrase as it should be made, I can only condole with her and remind her of the existence of the fireplace, where she has my leave to burn these pages. ... But how I envy her the task I am preparing for her! ... The lady of 50 will be able to say how near to the truth I come.'

Her diary was an exercise book for her literary thoughts. In it she not only reviewed the books she read, but ordered her thoughts on the books she was going to write. One can track the development of her novel *To The Lighthouse* over two years, beginning on May 14th 1925: 'I'm now all on the strain with desire to ... get on to *To the Lighthouse*. This is going to be fairly short: to have father's character done complete in it; & mothers; & St Ives; & childhood; & all the usual things I try to put in—life, death &c. But the centre is father's character, sitting in a boat, reciting We perished, each alone, while he crushes a dying mackerel ...'

The onset of World War Two brought on a resurgence of her anxiety and depression. Death, of which she so often wrote, seemed to be all around her. 'Walking today by Kingfisher pool saw my first hospital train – laden, not funereal but weighty, as if not to shake bones: something ... –bringing our wounded back carefully through the green fields at which I suppose some looked. ... The slowness, cadaverousness, grief of the long heavy train, taking its burden through the fields.'

Her final diary entry, on March 24th 1941, recorded a meeting with a neighbour. 'Before 5 minutes had passed she told us that two of her sons had been killed in the war. ... Sitting there I tried to coin a few compliments. But they perished in the icy sea between us. And then there was nothing.' On March 28th, she committed suicide by walking into the fast-flowing River Ouse near her home, with heavy stones in her pockets.

LEFT: Virginia Woolf, considered one of the most influential writers of her generation. Today, her works have been translated into more than fifty languages and are read across the world.

Harry S. Truman, 33rd President of the United States

(1884–1972)

With Harry S. Truman on the ticket, Franklin D. Roosevelt swept all before him in the US presidential election of 1944. When he died only three months after being sworn in for a record fourth term, Truman was left holding the reins of a country at war, and with an option to use an atomic bomb.

Only a year earlier, in March 1944, Truman had become aware of the enormous expense of America's Manhattan Project to develop the A-bomb, and had begun to ask questions about its value to the taxpayer's dollar. He was warned off by Henry Stimson, the US Secretary of War and backed down. America had been at war with Japan since the attack on Pearl Harbor in 1941, and since then Roosevelt had also been drawn into the European war against Germany. From its inception, the Manhattan Project had been seen as a way of ending, either by its potential threat or by its actual usage, the Japanese war – and potentially all wars subsequent.

We now know that the possibility of nuclear annihilation is not enough to discourage warmongers; and when it became clear to Truman that Japan would fight to the bitter end rather than surrender, he was forced to consider the possibility of detonating such a bomb. The Trinity Test in New Mexico, the first attempt to do so, took place on July 16th 1945, the day before Truman travelled to Potsdam to meet the leaders of the Soviet Union and Great Britain, where they intended to discuss the future of Europe – Nazi Germany had surrendered a month into Truman's presidency.

Truman believed that the success of the test gave America a stronger hand in negotiations, and could hardly wait to tell Stalin, the Soviet Union's representative. On the first day of the Potsdam Conference, July 17th, Truman wrote in his diary, 'I asked him if he had the agenda for the meeting. He said he had and that he had some more questions to present. I told him to fire away. He did and it is dynamite – but I have some dynamite too, which I am not exploding now.'

Truman did so when the time was right, in a meeting with Stalin on July 24th; Stalin seemed unimpressed, and his only reply was that 'he was glad to hear of the bomb and he hoped we would use it.' Unknown to Truman, Stalin already knew about it through his intelligence network.

The next day, Truman's diary noted the scale of the destruction in the New Mexico tests - 'a crater six hundred deep and twelve hundred feet in diameter' - and reflected on the awful decision he must make. 'We have discovered,' he wrote, 'the most terrible bomb in the history of the world.'

Truman, the only US president in the twentieth century not to hold a college degree, was alarmed about the possibility of civilian casualties. 'I have told the Secretary of War Mr Stinson to use it so that military objectives and soldiers and sailors are the target.'

In the event, the bombs could not discriminate; and Truman acknowledged that 'it is certainly a good thing for the world that Hitler's crowd or Stalin's did not discover the atomic bomb. It seems to be the most terrible thing ever discovered.'

ABOVE: Truman, photographed in 1947, at the outset of the Cold War.

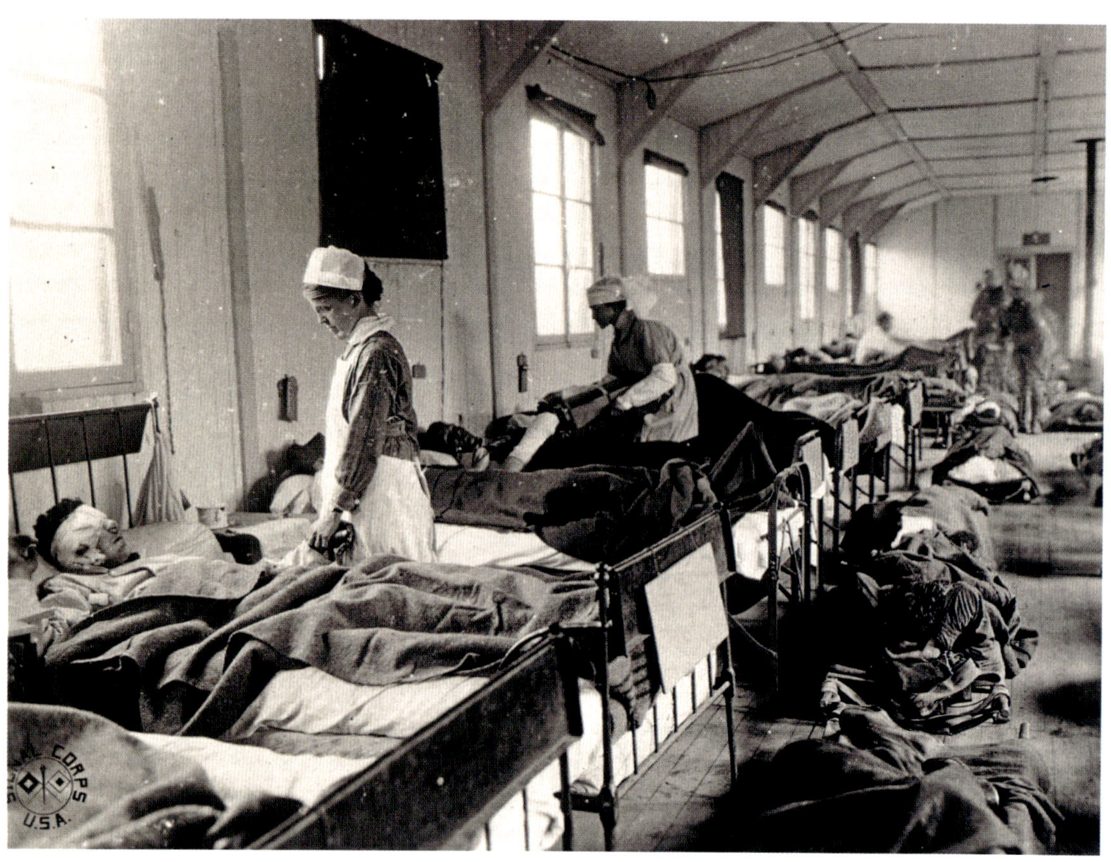

ABOVE: Kit McNaughton was one of thousands of women who served as wartime nurses. Her diaries were later used as the basis for the book Kitty's War *by Janet Butler almost a century later.*

Kit McNaughton, Australian wartime nurse

(1887–1953)

Catherine "Kit" McNaughton answered the call, along with 2,500 others, to enlist in 1915 as nurses treating the wounded of World War One. Her wartime diaries have helped to publicise the under-appreciated role and disparaging treatment of women in conflict.

After a brief spell behind the lines in Cairo, McNaughton's baptism of fire came in a field hospital on the Greek island of Lemnos, from where she could hear the guns of Gallipoli which had injured her hundreds of patients. The notoriously costly campaign there against the Ottoman Empire took a high toll on ANZAC forces; and Kit, from a small town in Victoria, was there to patch them up.

She and the group of nurses who travelled with her to Lemnos were naturally excited about their posting to a hospital of bell tents on the island. At first, the injuries which came to them were slight. The tone of McNaughton's diary began to change however as the wounds became more serious and the injured more numerous. When she recorded that another 200 injured were about to arrive she remarked, 'God help them.'

Resources were scarce, manpower scarcer – and the medical orderlies assigned to them were soldiers first, with a mere three weeks training at a hospital in Perth. The injured were more likely to respond to their superior officers than to the women – whom many older soldiers considered an unnecessary complication in the field. The soldier's rations were cut and their living conditions cold, damp and unsanitary. McNaughton described the nurses' habit of sitting on the edge of their beds at night picking the lice out of their clothing which they had caught from their patients. For the rest of her life McNaughton was plagued by the illnesses from which she had contracted on Lemnos.

Life was cheap, but in one instance McNaughton's intervention saved the life of one young man whom she recognised from her home town and who had been consigned to the mortuary ward where the untreatable were left to die. As the action in the Dardanelles came to an end the nurses were pleased to be leaving Lemnos; but worse was to come. McNaughton was posted to a field hospital in France just as the military madness of the Battle of the Somme commenced, in which on the first day alone 58,000 allied troops were killed out of the 100,000 that Lord Kitchener directed at the German positions.

Her compassion became dulled by the sheer scale of her task; yet it is an extraordinary mark of the persistence of humanity in the face of such hellish events as the Somme, that McNaughton found herself treating German casualties as well as allied ones. 'I have eleven with their legs off,' she wrote on one ordinary day, 'and a cuple [sic] ditto arms & hips & heads galore & the awful smell from the wounds is the limit as this Gas Gangrene is the most awful thing imaginable, a leg goes in a day. I extracted a bullet from a German's back today, and I enjoyed cutting into him ... the bullet is my small treasure, as I hope it saved a life as it was a revolver one.'

McNaughton could tell one bullet from another. She could operate surgically, something which a nurse would never be asked to do in peacetime. Her anger with the authorities sometimes boiled over, and she was nearly cashiered on one occasion. But Kit was also commended in dispatches, and after the war she was awarded a Royal Red Cross Medal First Class for her life-saving work.

R. H. Bruce Lockhart, British secret agent

(1887–1970)

In 1908 Robert Bruce Lockhart set out from his Scottish home to seek his fortune as a rubber planter in Malaya, but after three years he was stricken with malaria. Changing course, he sought entry into the UK Consular Service, where his career took an entirely different path.

A young Robert, always referred to by his initials R. H., was the best candidate in his year. He was selected to be the British Vice Consul in Moscow, climbing the ranks to become the Acting Consul General before he was thirty. He was recalled to London early in 1917 but was back ten months later as Head of the UK Mission to the provisional Communist Government.

By this time Bruce Lockhart had been keeping a diary for three years. He handwrote it, with some of the entries in a personal shorthand or in Malay, when he was writing about marital difficulties or concerns about his partying and his drinking. This was the raw material for his later memoirs, particularly his *Memoirs of a British Agent* (1932), although the deepest secrets, the intelligence work with Sidney Reilly, for example, are not recorded in the diary. However, the journal does give impressions of some of the figures he did business with: Lenin, Trotsky, and the Head of the Secret Police (the Cheka) Feliks Djerjinsky described as 'a man of correct manners and quiet speech without a ray of humour in his character.'

In September Bruce Lockhart was arrested by the Bolsheviks for allegedly conspiring to assassinate Lenin and for cheating Trotsky in respect of the Allied intervention in Russia earlier in 1918. Lockhart's diary describes his cell in the Kremlin as a small and heavily guarded apartment. 'I have one sentry on one side and two on the other. They are changed every four hours and as each changes, he has to come in and see if I am there. This results in me being woken up at twelve and four in the middle of the night.'

R. H. was in the cell for a month before a hasty deal got him back to the UK. As he packed up his personal possessions, he discovered corruption at first hand. 'My pearl studs, my heart pin and about a hundred or two hundred roubles have been stolen. The soldiers also drank all our wine, stole our butter and flour.'

The journals for 1920 to 1924 are missing, perhaps destroyed for security reasons, but Bruce Lockhart's life remained frenzied. First, he engaged in diplomatic service in Czechoslovakia then out of the service into banking and then journalism – as a gossip columnist. He continued to wine and dine, meeting with most of the London elite during the 1930s, among them Mrs Simpson (described as 'the Prince of Wales's girl'). Lockhart's friendship with the minister Anthony Eden led, in 1942 to his becoming Director General of the Political Warfare Executive. After the war, he returned to writing and kept a journal for the rest of his life.

RIGHT: British secret agents have long been sensationalised in popular media. This image is an advertising postcard for the popular wartime play and spy-thriller The Man Who Stayed at Home *from c. 1914.*

PUZZLE:
FIND THE
GERMAN SPY.

ABOVE: Nella Last and her youngest son, Clifford. As well as being a housewife and mother, Nella volunteered for the Women's Voluntary Service and the British Red Cross during the Second World War.

Nella Last, English Housewife and Mass Observation participant

(1889-1968)

Britain's Mass Observation Project was set up in 1937 by a group of former students, as a way of studying the lives of ordinary people. The project appealed for people to keep and submit daily diaries and among the 480 who responded was Nella Last, who started her diary in 1939 with the words 'Housewife, 49.'

Nella continued to write the diary until 1966 when she was seventy-six, one of the longest diaries ever written in English, at more than 12 million words. She was married with two sons. Her husband was a joiner and they lived in Barrow-in-Furness, a ship-building town which was a regular target for German bombing raids.

During the war, Nella volunteered for various women's institutions. One of her sons, Cliff, fought in India and Italy where he was wounded. Nella empathised with mothers from Barrow to Berlin. 'I look round at faces I have known and loved for over four years,' she wrote in 1943 of her fellow volunteers. 'My heart aches [for their] bravery and courage, the "going on" when only sons have been killed, when letters don't come, when their boys are trained and trained and trained. To go and kill other women's lads, to wipe all the light from other mother's faces.'

Through the course of her diary, Nella came to realise that she had a way with words. 'I'm beginning to see that I'm really a clever woman in my own line, and not the "uneducated" woman that I've had dinned into me. In the World of tomorrow, marriage will be - have to be - more of a partnership. They will talk things over - talking does do good, if only to clear the air.'

One of the narrative threads of her diary was an acceptance that she is a woman, a person, in her own right. Nella was becoming aware of the "maleness" of the world. 'Men do seem to get the best out of life,' she wrote. And when Cliff came home on leave in early 1941, she was in no mood to put up with it. 'I gave Cliff a very big helping as he had to catch the train back [to his base] after lunch. He said, "If you ever have to work for a living Mum, come and cook for the Army." I said, "... I guess a married woman who brings up a family and makes a home, is working jolly hard for her living. And don't you ever forget it. And don't get the lordly male attitude of thinking wives are pets - and kept pets at that."'

By the time of the German surrender in 1945, Nella had a very different perspective on her marriage. 'I looked at [my husband's] placid blank face and marvelled at the way he had managed so to dominate me for all our married life, at how, to avoid hurting him, I had tried to keep him in a good mood ... with nerves kept in control ... and nervous breakdowns were the result. No one would ever give me one again, no one. ... I can never go back to that harem existence that my husband thinks so desirable.'

Forty years after completion Last's account of her life during World War Two was dramatized movingly for television by English writer Victoria Wood, under the title *Housewife, 49*.

Bella Fromm, German wartime diarist and journalist

(1890–1972)

When is a diary not a diary? Recent research suggests that Bella Fromm's diaries of social life in Germany's Weimar Republic were in fact written retrospectively after she had fled Nazi Germany, for the safety of the USA. Perhaps a contentious inclusion, diaries form the basis for many biographies and memoirs, often suitably revised with hindsight.

The Weimar Republic, so called because the conference which brought it into being at the end of World War One was held in the German city of Weimar, came to an end with the appointment of Adolf Hitler as Chancellor in 1933. Bella Fromm was Jewish, and a diplomatic correspondent in Berlin for several newspapers including *The Times*. Her family were successful wine merchants.

As Hitler first banned Jews from writing under their own name, and then barred them from involvement in the wider trade of publishing, Bella had no choice but to escape to America in 1938. There she published *Blood and Banquets*, an account of life during the Republic, when she had mixed in the highest political and social circles. Her family were friends of the Bavarian royals; and in the context of diplomatic dinners with the ambassadors of many European countries she also met the men who would become the engineers of Germany's Third Reich - Hermann Göring, Rudolf Hess, Joseph Goebbels and Hitler himself.

In her introduction to *Blood and Banquets*, Fromm was at pains to state that 'In preparing this book, I made excerpts from the original entries in my diary. ... The parts of my diary which are contained in this book stand just as they were originally written.' A comparison of the various drafts of her original manuscript disproves this, since the quoted diary passages often underwent considerable revision from one draft to the next. There are some errors of date and place which she would have been unlikely to make at the time – for example, a major speech by Hitler which she placed on January 27th 1932 when it was actually given on the 26th. Doubt has been cast too on the likelihood of her being on first-name terms with Kurt von Schleicher, Hitler's predecessor as Chancellor.

Historians have been advised to consult *Blood and Banquets* with scepticism. However, there is no doubt about the general authenticity of Frau Fromm's experiences, even if she did tamper with the articulation of them. The diaries chart with grim inevitability the rise of Hitler to power. Her thumbnail sketch of an awkward, nervous Hitler making his debut in diplomatic society is comically described in an entry for February 10th 1933. 'The corporal seemed to be ill at ease, awkward and moody. His coattails embarrassed him. Again and again he fumbled for the encouraging support of his sword belt. He crumpled his handkerchief, tugged it, rolled it, just plain stage fright.'

Fromm's diaries chart the horrors of Hitler's progress to power with candid cynicism and although there is plenty of disturbing reportage, Fromm finds time for dry humour at Hitler's expense. 'I hear Hitler absolutely declines to have his speeches recorded on sound films,' she notes. 'A member of the foreign press asked Brueckner, his adjutant, for the reason. "You can't alter a sound film," he said.'

To answer the original question, Hitler's own diaries, "discovered" in 1983 and sold to *Die Stern* magazine for 9.3 million Deutschmarks, proved to be the work of a petty forger of Nazi memorabilia.

Norddeutsche Ausgabe / Ausgabe A

31. Ausg. • 46. Jahrg. • Einzelpreis 20 Pf.

Freiheit und Brot

Ausgabe A / Norddeutsche Ausgabe

Berlin, Dienstag, 31. Januar 1933

VÖLKISCHER BEOBACHTER

Herausgeber Adolf Hitler

Kampfblatt der national-sozialistischen Bewegung Großdeutschlands

Ein historischer Tag:

Erste Maßnahmen der Reichsregierung Hitler

Interview des „Völkischen Beobachters" mit dem Reichsinnenminister Frick – Tagung des neuen Kabinetts

Der Reichspräsident von Hindenburg hat Adolf Hitler zum Reichskanzler ernannt. Der neuen Regierung werden neben Adolf Hitler als Reichskanzler der frühere Minister Pg. Frick als Reichsinnenminister und der Reichstagspräsident Pg. Goering als Reichsminister ohne Geschäftsbereich und Reichskommissar für den Luftverkehr angehören. Pg. Goering wird gleichzeitig mit der Wahrnehmung der Geschäfte des Preußischen Innenministeriums betraut.

ADOLF HITLER

Reichsinnenminister Dr. Frick

Reichsminister Goering

Berlin, 30. Januar.

Die im Anschluß an die Ernennung Adolf Hitlers herausgegebene amtliche Mitteilung hat folgenden Wortlaut:

„Der Reichspräsident hat Herrn Adolf Hitler zum Reichskanzler ernannt und auf dessen Vorschlag die Reichsregierung wie folgt neu gebildet:

Reichskanzler a. D. von Papen zum Stellvertreter des Kanzlers und Reichskommissar für das Land Preußen;

Freiherrn von Neurath zum Reichsminister des Auswärtigen;

Staatsminister a. D. M. d. R. Dr. Frick zum Reichsminister des Innern;

Generalleutnant Freiherrn von Blomberg zum Reichswehrminister;

Graf von Schwerin-Krosigk zum Reichsminister der Finanzen;

Geheimen Finanzrat M. d. R. Hugenberg zum Reichsminister der Wirtschaft und zum Reichsminister für Ernährung und Landwirtschaft;

Franz Seldte zum Reichsarbeitsminister;

Freiherrn von Eltz-Rübenach zum Reichspostminister und zum Reichsverkehrsminister;

Reichstagspräsidenten Goering zum Reichsminister ohne Geschäftsbereich und gleichzeitig zum Reichskommissar für den Luftverkehr.

Reichsminister Goering wurde mit der Wahrnehmung der Geschäfte des Preußischen Innenministeriums betraut.

Reichskommissar für Arbeitsbeschaffung Gereke wird in seinem Amt bestätigt.

Die Besetzung des Reichsjustizministeriums bleibt vorbehalten. Der Reichskanzler wird noch heute Verhandlungen mit dem Zentrum und der Bayerischen Volkspartei aufnehmen. Heute nachmittag 17 Uhr findet die erste Kabinettssitzung statt."

Das Ziel der neuen Regierung:

Die geistige und willensmäßige Erneuerung des deutschen Volkes

Erklärt Reichsinnenminister Dr. Frick in einer Unterredung mit dem „Völkischen Beobachter"

Sollte sich dies die Kommunistische Partei nicht noch anders überlegen, so werden wir mit den schärfsten Maßnahmen gegen einen derartigen Generalstreik vorgehen."

Die Richtung unserer Politik deckt sich mit unserer bisherigen nationalsozialistischen Stellungnahme zu dieser Frage.

„Es wurde mir mitgeteilt, Herr Minister, …

Der Grundstein zum Dritten Reich

Der 30. Januar 1933 wird einmal eingehen in die Geschichtsschreibung als ein Tag, der einen historischen Umschwung der deutschen Entwicklung darstellt. …

Stürmische Huldigungen

Nationalsozialistische Staatssekretäre in Preußen

Flaggen heraus!

ABOVE: A Nazi newspaper, the People's Observer, announces on January 31st 1933 'the first measures of the Hitler government'. Bella Fromm, a Jewish journalist in Berlin, fled the country in 1938, a year before the start of World War Two.

Vera Brittain, English author and pacifist

(1893–1970)

Author of the autobiographical novel *Testament of Youth* Vera Brittain based the work on the diaries which she kept during World War One. The diaries themselves, published posthumously, are no less literary and a far more immediate response to the horrors which were unfolding around her.

By the time she wrote *Testament of Youth*, in 1933, Vera Brittain was embracing the pacifism which would guide the rest of her life. During World War Two she campaigned actively against the indiscriminate saturation bombing of German towns and cities, for which she is remembered in the name of a street in Hamburg, Vera-Brittain-Ufer.

Vera's World War One diaries are a record of the reactions and tragic events which guided her toward an eventual anti-war stance. The commitment which Brittain felt in 1933 was only embryonic during that first conflict, which was punctuated by four heart-stopping lightning bolts – the deaths in battle of her fiancé Roland Leighton, two dear friends Victor Richardson and Geoffrey Thurlow, and her brother Edward. The loss of Edward haunted Vera for the rest of her life, and in her will she asked for her ashes to be scattered on his grave in Italy, because 'for nearly 50 years much of my heart has been in that Italian village cemetery.'

At the outbreak of the war, she was swept along by the wave of patriotism and excitement shared by many in Britain. Leighton and her brother were among thousands who volunteered for military service, and Brittain herself abandoned her university courses to serve as a nurse in a Voluntary Aid Detachment, serving the war effort in England, Malta and France. 'When I read [Roland's] first letter from the trenches,' she wrote to Edward, two months after her fiancé's death, 'it made me wish desperately that I were a man and could train myself to play that "Great Game with Death".'

Roland's death came with cruel timing. 'I found a tiny note from Roland,' her diary noted on December 17th 1915, 'saying simply "Leave from 24th – 31st. Land on Christmas Day." I was wildly thrilled ... and greatly troubled lest something should happen in the meantime to stop it, as other people's leaves have been stopped.' She prayed in church on Christmas Day for Roland's safe return.

And then on December 27th Vera wrote, 'a message came to say that there was a telephone message for me. I sprang up joyfully, thinking to hear in a moment the dear, dreamed-of tones of the beloved voice. Unfortunately, the telephone message came not from Roland but from Claire. It was not to say that Roland had arrived, but that instead had come a telegram that explained Roland had been shot by a sniper and died of his wounds on December 23rd.

Brittain's wartime diaries end before the death of her brother, and she then transferred from Malta to a field hospital at Étaples in France, close to the action, where she felt genuinely useful. As she confessed on May 27th 1917, '[It] made me very glad I had elected to be a nurse and remained one, instead of doing something else.'

LEFT: Vera Brittain, seen aboard the Carinthia boat train on her way to meet her husband in Montreal in 1956.

Noël Coward, English playwright and composer

(1899–1973)

A quintessential Englishman of his times – snobbish, understated, aloof – Noël Coward's public persona was all the things which he encouraged his audience to laugh at about themselves. The same characteristics inform his eloquently written diaries, where his humour often masked real concern.

If one had to typify a Noël Coward diary entry, it would read something like this: 'Daphne and Boy Browning came for drinks - long talk to Daphne about Gertie. She loved her very much. Then Larry and Vivien arrived and we all went to Douglas Fairbanks' dinner party for Charlie Chaplin ... After dinner more people arrived - I obliged at the pianoforte - Mary Martin came to my rescue and we sang together.'

This extended orgy of name-dropping is from his diary of September 27th 1952. For the uninitiated, Daphne was the novelist Daphne du Maurier, married to army veteran Lt-Gen Sir Frederick "Boy" Browning; Gertie was Gertrude Lawrence, an actor for whom Coward wrote many parts and songs; and Larry and Vivien were the golden couple of British theatre, Sir Lawrence Olivier and his wife Vivien Leigh. This is exactly how one can imagine Coward spending his time, in one long celebrity-strewn party where his flamboyant wit could be centre-stage.

At the outbreak of World War Two however, Coward – then in his fortieth year – turned his back on theatre and looked for ways in which he could be useful to the war effort. He was at first engaged by Britain's Secret Service to run their Paris propaganda bureau, in the hope that his celebrity would encourage the United States to support Britain. To the British public however, it looked as if Noël was enjoying a spot of foreign travel while they were suffering from shortages at home.

The Prime Minister Winston Churchill decided that Coward would be better employed entertaining the troops, telling him to "go and sing to them when the guns are firing – that's your job!' Although one might imagine that the debonair doyen of high society would have been horrified at the thought of appearing anywhere except a theatre in London's West End, Coward embraced this new role.

Inevitably he underplayed the dangers and over-egged the social side of life, even in war. Coward once described a visit to the quarters of an old acquaintance, Richard Casey, a member of Churchill's war cabinet, on September 20th 1943 somewhere in Northern Africa.

Casey's security detail was a battalion of Gurkhas who executed their duties with considerable zeal. 'These sentries have been known to fly at Dick himself and pin him into the car with their bayonets until he remembered the right password.' Coward ensured his own safety by 'shrieking the password whenever I entered the gate and cringing submissively'.

Coward performed on makeshift stages in aircraft hangars and hospitals. Mindful of the public's reaction to his time in Paris, he tried to stop patients taking photographs of him, for fear it would look as if he was attracting publicity 'at the expense of the wounded men. However the matron explained to me that the men liked the photography because they could get copies and send them home to their wives, so I let it go.'

RIGHT: Noël Coward passed away in 1972. In 2006 the former Albery Theatre was renamed after Coward in his honor.

Heinrich Himmler, German Nazi and commander of the SS

(1900–1945)

The man who conducted the Holocaust with the avowed intention of 'eliminating the Jews' took his own life rather than face punishment after World War Two. The recent discovery of his diaries raised hopes of an insight into the mind of a monster.

Himmler's journals were among thousands of documents looted by advancing Soviet forces at the end of the war. Himmler himself was on the run, having fallen out of favour with Adolf Hitler for trying to negotiate with the Allies when defeat became inevitable. The papers were brought back to Moscow and Himmler's notebooks, labelled in a hurry by an archivist merely as "Diaries", were forgotten about for almost seventy years, until they were more accurately identified in 2013.

To the disappointment of some, they are not personal records of Himmler's feelings. The accounts are not expressions of satisfaction in his work, and certainly not of any remorse for his actions. The "diaries" are not even in his handwriting – they are the dictated record of the events of each day, typed up afterwards by his office staff. In any other context the pages would be the rather dull desk diary of any business executive; but Himmler's business was mass murder. As one of his entries explains, 'It is one of those things that is easily said. "The Jewish people is being exterminated," every Party member will tell you, "Perfectly clear, it's part of our plans, we're eliminating the Jews, exterminating them, a small matter."'

What strikes time and again when reading Himmler's diaries is the equanimity with which he records all the news of the day. A delicious meal with fellow officers is reported in the same terms as a visit to a concentration camp. Family matters are dealt with in the same tone as execution orders. 'Tea and agreement to become godfather to his son,' he reminds himself after a dinner with Fritz Sauckel, who would later be hanged for his part in the merciless use of prisoners as slave labour. A typical day might begin with breakfast followed by a massage from his personal doctor, then a phone call home to his wife and daughter in Bavaria, before going on to inspect another concentration camp.

He was, no doubt, convinced that he was just doing his day job as efficiently and well as he could, before going home to the wife and kids. One day Himmler finds that he has left one of the day's tasks undone. He had been told earlier that some Polish policemen are refusing to fight for Nazi Germany; the day's diary concludes with '9–10 pm: Orders all ten officers be executed and their families sent to concentration camps before going to bed.'

On another day there has been a failure of organisation. Himmler is visiting a new diesel-powered gas chamber at a concentration camp in Poland, but no Jews have been scheduled for extermination that day. Himmler has to wait while troops round up 400 women and children from the nearby Lublin Ghetto, so that he can see the chamber in action. Afterwards he is the guest of honour at a banquet hosted by the camp's commandant. Himmler's lack of empathy is chilling.

LEFT : Himmler's General Plan Ost, approved in 1942, led to the deaths of 14 million people in Eastern Europe. He died by suicide in 1945 while in British custody.

Petter Moen, Norwegian newspaper editor

(1901–1944), as translated by Bjorn Koefoed

Some diaries are written by hand; others are typed; and some are made by piercing hard toilet paper with a pin to prick out the letters of the words. Petter Moen's prison diary is an essential record of the mental and physical torture of incarceration.

Petter Moen was an actuary, but when Germany occupied neutral Norway in 1940, he joined the Resistance. His role was one of communication: he edited *London-Nytt*, one of several underground newspapers which helped to coordinate acts of sabotage and passive resistance to the large occupying presence, roughly one German soldier for every eight Norwegians.

London-Nytt was published secretly for nearly three years and produced 540 editions. When Germany discovered the existence of it and other covert newspapers in February 1944, Moen and many of his associates were arrested and held at Møllergata 19, an Oslo police station which the German secret service had made its own.

Moen was imprisoned there for 216 days, the first seventy-eight of them in solitary confinement where he was subjected to interrogation and torture. The brutality and the isolation were intense, and to preserve his sanity he distracted himself with complex mathematical problems.

Petter was not a soldier, and his torturers broke his spirit. However, he was still a newspaper editor, and believed in the importance of recording facts. Deprived of everything except food he used what he could find – a pin from the blackout curtains, and toilet paper. Working in the darkness of the night, when he could neither see what he was writing nor review it, Moen scratched out the details of what he was enduring. He numbered each sheet, and when he had completed five of these he rolled them up in a protective sixth piece and hid them in a narrow airduct which led under the floorboards.

The diaries make for harrowing reading. 'From the 7th day of my prison stay at Møllergata 19,' he managed to write in February 1944. 'Have been in 2 interrogations. Was flogged. Betrayed Vic. Am weak. Deserve contempt. Am terribly scared of pain. But not scared to die.'

Similar to many people in crisis, Moen's thoughts turned to religion, although he struggled to reconcile his ideas of a God with his present predicament. In this existential torment, he was racked with guilt for having cracked under his violent treatment. 'I must recognize with bitter and painful regret how inexpressibly badly I have lived. ... I have reduced to dust all moral and material values.'

In early September 1944, he and his fellow prisoners were herded onto a ship, the *SS Westfalen*, to be transported to Germany. By then Moen had written and hidden over a thousand sheets, an act of will and an effort to make sense of what was happening to him. As the ship set sail, he told a fellow prisoner about the diary and its location, although neither of them likely believed that they would survive what awaited them in a German prison camp.

In the end, the *SS Westfalen* struck two mines on September 7th and sank quickly. Most of the German crew survived; but all but five of the Norwegian prisoners, trapped in the hold, were drowned. Moen died; but his confidant was rescued and after the war he was able to lead the authorities to Moen's remarkable record.

ABOVE: Petter Moen was imprisoned at Møllergata 19 when Nazi occupiers discovered he was working for an underground newspaper. It was during this imprisonment that he wrote his diary.

John Steinbeck, American author

(1902–1968)

The author of some of the greatest American Novels captured his country at a dire time in its history, during the Great Depression of the 1930s. As Steinbeck set out to *The Grapes of Wrath*, in 1938, he decided to keep a diary of its creation, the better to understand his writing process.

Of Mice and Men was published in 1937 and brought John Steinbeck his greatest success to date. There was, naturally eager anticipation for his next book. Steinbeck felt the pressure, but also had the sense of possibility. He began the diary on May 31st 1938, and on June 9th he described the task ahead. 'This must be a good book. It simply must. I haven't any choice. It must be far and away the best thing I have ever attempted - slow but sure, piling detail on detail until a picture and an experience emerge. Until the whole throbbing thing emerges. And I can do it. I feel very strong to do it.'

As a rule, Steinbeck wrote his novels quickly once the story and themes were clear in his mind. 'I have seven months to do this book,' he wrote on the first day, 'and I should like to take them but I imagine five will be the limit. I have never taken long actually to do the writing. I want this one to be leisurely though. That is one of the reasons for the diary.' By consciously observing his writing process, Steinbeck hoped to savour it.

The diary acted as a sounding board for the development of his novel, and at the end of the first month he was satisfied with progress, although he still felt he was writing too quickly. 'My system of time has indeed collapsed. Today - the last day of June I have finished in one month Book One, the background of this novel.' There was always a sense of the whole, however – an overview of where the story should be heading. 'I went over the whole of the book in my head - fixed on that last scene, huge and symbolic, toward which the whole story moves. And that was a good thing, for it was a reunderstanding of the dignity of the effort and the mightiness of the theme.'

As the novel progressed John became more and more certain of its possible greatness. 'I felt very small and inadequate and incapable but I grew again to love the story which is so much greater than I am. To love and admire the people who are so much stronger and purer and braver than I am.' The diary gives the sense that the novel existed, fully formed inside him, and that his job as a writer was to do it justice in the writing of it.

Doubts about his ability to do so were never far away. After three months, on August 29th, he chided himself. 'Now I have lost a great deal of time. I have been remiss and lazy. ... But I am always this way. I can concentrate and under some circumstances, I can work. My job is to get down to it and now. There is only one person to blame for all the pressures, and I must force him into it.' Despite his self-flagellation, he was by this time halfway through the book.

Five months after starting, the end was in sight. 'Today should be a day of joy because I could finish today,' he reported on October 26th. 'But I seem to have contracted an influenza. ... I'm so dizzy I can hardly see the page. ... I must go on.' Steinbeck's disciplined work ethic and his belief in the power of his story drove him onwards; and at the end of that day he noted, 'Finished this day - and hope to god it's good.'

LEFT : John Steinbeck won the Nobel Prize in Literature in 1962. His books are still taught in many schools and colleges around the world.

Evelyn Waugh, English novelist

(1903–1966)

The author of *Brideshead Revisited*, and many other novels, had a private reputation for kindness and generosity. In public however, Evelyn cultivated the persona of an irascible old army officer and enjoyed playing up to it. He kept a diary from the age of seven until a year before his death.

His grumpy image was well established by the end of World War Two. On March 6th 1946, he noted with unabashed sexism that he'd received 'an offensive letter from a female American Catholic. I returned it to her husband with the note: "I shall be grateful if you will use whatever disciplinary means are customary in your country to restrain your wife from writing impertinent letters to men she does not know."'

As his global fame increased, he was expected to be internationally offensive. He described a day's filming for American television on June 30th 1955.

The question of his irritability came up during the filming. 'The impresario kept producing notes from his pocket: "Mr Waugh, it is said here that you are irascible and reactionary. Will you please say something offensive?" So I said: "The man who has brought this apparatus to my house asks me to be offensive. I am sorry to disappoint him." "Oh, Mr Waugh, please, that will never do. I have a reputation. You must alter that."'

In adult life, Waugh kept his journal as a reminder of interesting characters and situations with which to fill his novels. Many of his later works draw on his own experiences as a journalist or as a soldier. Toward the end of the war he was posted to Yugoslavia, where Britain was wooing the local resistance groups led by Tito. Its rival was Russia, and after the war Tito, a committed communist, led the country while keeping both Britain and the Soviet Union at arm's length.

Waugh had more personal concerns. Life's little luxuries were in short supply, as an entry for July 14th 1944 showed. "Last cigar. As a result I am consumed with hunger and find myself popping furtively into the snack bar and eating sausage rolls at all hours. We drove to a town beginning with P for luncheon at a black-market restaurant in what appeared to be a private house. Tough tagliatelle, delicious little fish, nauseating zabaglione made I think with stolen American ice-cream powder."

Waugh's health, wealth and popularity declined toward the end of his life and his later diaries show him spending time with old friends, the ones who knew his real character. The final entry, written on Easter Day 1965, reported with sadness the death of one of them, Phil Dunne. Waugh's affectionate portrait of him was written with that core of kindness and generosity. 'He was my age. I last saw him just before Christmas, elegant, gay, and I thought how little he had aged compared with myself. He was completely selfish without an element of conceit or self assertion, debonair, never boring, never morose; a finely controlled temptation to malice; chivalrous, with a sense of private honour uncommon nowadays. Waugh might almost have been writing his own obituary. He died exactly a year later, on Easter Day, 1966.

ABOVE: Waugh was the son of a publisher, and was himself a literary reviewer and author throughout his life.

Anaïs Nin, Cuban/French writer

(1903–1977)

'Ordinary life does not interest me. I seek only the high moments. I am in accord with the surrealists, searching for the marvellous.' Anais Nin's diaries did not so much witness history as make it, by their publication. Six decades of candid sexual and psychological introspection record the lows, as well as the highs, of her life.

Anaïs Nin began to keep a diary at the age of seven. The account began as an appeal, in the form of a letter, asking her absconding father to return to the family and very soon it became her habit to explore her inner needs and feelings through the diary's pages. Typed up, the collected entries of her journal ran to 15,000 pages in 150 volumes in 1966, the year they were first published.

Nin's diary became her best friend, the one place where she could confide everything. Although acquaintances, psychiatrists and lovers sometimes tried to break her bond with it, she continued to write a diary until her death in 1977. It became apparent to Nin in the 1940s that, although she had written novels and short stories by then, her diary was the creative masterpiece of her life. The diary may have begun as a search for her father, and for father figures – the list of her lovers in the 1930s alone includes the authors Henry Miller and Lawrence Durrell: and her psychiatrists René Allendy and Otto Rank, but it eventually became a quest for a truly feminine worldview, not one shaped and dictated by men.

In a long discussion with Miller and Durrell one evening in August 1937 she began to try to articulate her position, that after first defining the world from a male perspective, man then claimed to be objective in his view of it. 'Man fabricated a detachment which became fatal. ... Man invented a woman to suit his needs. He disposed of her by identifying her with nature and then paraded his contemptuous domination of nature.'

Woman, she insisted, 'has to create something different from man. Man created a world cut off from nature. Woman has to create within the mystery, storms, terrors, the infernos of sex, the battle against abstractions and art.' Nin did not argue for feminist separation from men, acknowledging instead the role of men in the creation of both men and women. 'What will be marvelous to contemplate,' she wrote, ' will not be her solitude but this image of woman being visited at night by man and the marvellous things she will give birth to in the morning.'

Nin's ideas of feminism coalesced when in the winter of 1942 she began to see therapist Martha Jaeger in New York. Having been the lover of many men, including briefly her own father, twenty years after he walked out on his family, she was now exhausting herself, 'trying to mother the entire world,' as she put it. Jaeger helped her to step back and reassess. 'This is a new drama,' Nin told her diary. She had dealt with the external drama of woman's relationship with man. Now she confronted an internal tension. 'The father is absent from this drama. This one is the drama of the mother, of woman. ... I have had all my relationships with men, of all kinds. Now my drama is that of the woman in relation to herself – her conflict between selfishness and individuality, and how to manifest the cosmic consciousness she feels.'

Anaïs Nin's diaries, landmarks of feminist thought and erotic candour, are available in two versions. During her lifetime she revised them for publication omitting, at his request, all references to her first husband, and self-censoring some of the most explicit entries and the fact that she was for time bigamously married to two men. After her death, her second husband authorised the publishing of most of the diaries in their unexpurgated, unrevised original form.

LEFT : French-born Anaïs lived at various times in Spain, Cuba and the United States. She kept a journal from her youth until her death in 1977.

Malcolm Muggeridge, English journalist and satirist

(1903–1990)

Few remember Malcolm Muggeridge today, but for a generation or two he was a fixture of British television chat shows and documentaries. Muggeridge's personal journey through left-wing politics, Christianity and journalism are charted by his lifelong habit of keeping a diary.

Muggeridge's father was a founder member of the British Labour Party and Muggeridge himself was attracted to communism – until he made a pilgrimage to Moscow in 1932. Muggeridge was an agnostic; but, witnessing the secular ritual of Russians queuing for hours to visit Vladimir Lenin's tomb on September 17th, he felt that something was missing: 'No one kisses the glass around him, or makes the sign of the Hammer and Sickle, or anything like that. They just stare. ... Coming away from the tomb I looked into a church and saw four or five old crones and a half-witted priest blessing one another indiscriminately. Christianity at least is over in Russia, and it is difficult to see how it will ever be revived.'

When he travelled to Ukraine, then suffering from a politically imposed famine which killed millions of Ukrainians, he became thoroughly disillusioned with the Russian Socialist experiment. 'Evil is the only apt word,' he wrote afterwards. 'Evil because there is no virtue in it; and because it has utterly failed.' His 1934 novel *Winter in Moscow* satirised the regime, and the willingness of the British press to turn a blind eye to it.

Malcolm first came to public attention with an iconoclastic newspaper article titled "Does England Really Need a Queen?" in 1955, two years after the coronation of Elizabeth II. From then on, he was a regular voice on chat shows where a controversial opinion was often required. He settled into the role of curmudgeonly critic of modern life, particularly of the values of the permissive society of the 1960s.

As early as August 1936 Muggeridge was beginning to question his agnosticism. 'I know that love governs the universe,' he admitted. 'I know that whatever success or ecstasy might be it would be dust and ashes unless I felt myself at one with God.' He became a Protestant in 1969; but, disillusioned by the Anglicanism he joined the Catholic church in 1982. Although much admired for his articulate intellect, he came off worst in a televised discussion with members of the *Monty Python* comedy team in 1979, about the merits of their religious satire *The Life of Brian*, which he found blasphemous.

For the public perception of Muggeridge toward the end of his life, we may turn to the (fictional) diary of another self-styled intellectual, Adrian Mole (age thirteen and three-quarters), who was the creation of novelist Sue Townsend.

'Sunday January 11th 1981. Now I know I am an intellectual. I saw Malcolm Muggeridge on the television last night, and I understood nearly every word.'

'Tuesday January 13th 1981. I have written to Malcolm Muggeridge, c/o the BBC, asking him what to do about being an intellectual.'

'Friday January 23rd 1981. I still haven't heard from Malcolm Muggeridge. Perhaps he is in a bad mood. Intellectuals like him and me often have bad moods.'

ABOVE : Muggeridge's diaries were published in 1981 under the title Like It Was.

Jean-Paul Sartre, French writer and philosopher

(1905–1980)

The French existentialist thinker and playwright Jean-Paul Sartre was not a habitual diarist, although he adopted the diary-form for his first novel *Nausea*, published in 1938. A year later, with the advent of war, Sartre was conscripted and kept a diary of his brief period of service in the French Army.

Sartre had completed his French military service ten years before the war. He had been assigned to the Meteorological Corps – the army's weather forecasters – and so in 1939 he was given the same occupation, stationed behind the front lines near Strasbourg. He had in the meantime become quite accustomed to the solitary, self-centred life of a writer; and the shock of joining not only a military unit but a social one, with other conscripts, amused him.

Although he expected to have no time for writing, his duties – taking a few weather readings every day – were light and allowed him more time than ever. In a few months Sartre had written a journal of a million words. The fourteen notebooks which he filled also contained drafts of letters and future novels. The fighting itself had not reached him and he had time to write at length about his life to date and his expectations for the future. 'I am giving myself short shrift in my little black notebook,' he wrote to his lover Simone de Beauvoir. 'Whoever reads it after my death—for you will publish it only posthumously—will think I was a dreadful character, unless you accompany it with explanatory annotations of a kindly sort.' They eventually found their way into print in 1985. Today Sartre is remembered as a contrarian, anti-authoritarian public public philosopher with a very liberal private life.

Naturally, Sartre's philosophical mind spent time considering the nature of war, particularly a "phoney" war in which no fighting was yet taking place. 'I found myself in contact with Corporal Paul,' he wrote on September 14th 1939. 'War is a form of socialism. It reduces man's individual property to nothing, and replaces it with collective property. My clothing, my bedding and my food no longer belong to me; I don't have a home any more. Everything I use belongs to the collective.'

He observed that the presence of war changed one's relationship with their environment, when finding himself on patrol one day near a beautiful oak wood. 'We had lain down on the edge of the road, crushed by our rifles, our backpacks, our greatcoats, like upside-down mayflies. I would have liked—not to go into the wood, but to think that I could do so.' To do so however would have meant breaking ranks, disobeying orders and risking death from a sniper. 'It was impossible to think such a thing, it lay outside my possibilities. ... By having ceased to be within my possibilities, these remote places lose their reality. The fellows here translate this by saying of a pleasant landscape or an agreeable village: "I'll come back when it's peacetime."'

Sartre's war ended suddenly with an unexpected German advance and his capture, from which he was released after nine months on health grounds. His war diaries are a rare insight into the development of his philosophy and his writing. He may have realised that diary-writing was not for him, and that his entries were not reliable. As the central character in *Nausea* observes, 'I think that is the big danger in keeping a diary: you exaggerate everything.'

LEFT Jean-Paul Sartre, Nobel Prize winner and French philosopher of the twentieth century.

Lord Longford, English politician and reformer

(1905-2001)

Frank Pakenham, Lord Longford, began making compassionate visits to prisoners in the 1930s, soon after entering politics as a local counsillor. He continued throughout his life and became a passionate campaigner for penal reform in Great Britain.

Frank Pakenham was a rarity in British politics – a hereditary peer from an aristocratic Anglo-Irish background who was not a natural supporter of the country's Conservative Party. Moreover, he served as a member of the Labour Party cabinet on several occasions, and remained active in politics until his death at the age of ninety-five.

Pakenham's reforming zeal was driven by his devout Christianity, and his often-cited rule of thumb was 'Hate the sin, love the sinner.' Thus, he was able to fight for the repeal of Britain's repressive laws against homosexuality while finding the practice incompatible with his beliefs; and he also campaigned for the early release of a convicted mass murderer, Myra Hindley, without condoning her crimes.

Two volumes of his diaries have been published to date. The first, *Diary of a Year*, was commissioned by his publisher to show the busy life of a hard-working politician during 1981. The second, *My Prison Diary*, contained extracts from his diaries from 1995 to 1999 as they pertained to his prison visits. They described the prisoners whom he met, and the sometimes-shocking conditions in which they were held.

Pakenham persisted in his belief that Myra Hindley was a reformed character and a remarkable woman. When giving a talk on November 22nd 1995 entitled *Christianity and Punishment* he explained 'as usual I was asked about Myra Hindley. What sort of woman was she? I caused some surprise by saying that she was probably as good a person as anyone in the room, except — I added as an afterthought — the priest sitting next to me.'

His relationship with her was sometimes the subject of gossip. 'He recalled, on April 11th 1997, being questioned about one of his visits to Hindley.. 'The prosecuting lawyer put it to me, "Would you say that you were under Miss Hindley's thrall, Lord Longford?" "That may or may not be so," I replied, "but at least the supervising officer was there to make sure that nothing untoward took place."'

Longford was convinced that public opinion, whipped up by the popular press, was the reason for Hindley's continued incarceration: the topic won votes for whichever party was in government. He fought a running battle with the tabloid newspapers, which persisted in demonising Hindley even thirty years after the murders, and in time became himself the target. When his support of Hindley was undermined by her belated confession that she had committed more murders than previously acknowledged, the papers dubbed him "Lord Wrongford".

On one of his last visits to Myra, on July 22nd 1998, Longford noted that 'she was happier than I ever remember her. She has a room, not a cell, and a piece of garden to herself. More importantly, she has found an inner peace through her religion.' It may be that Longford, nearing the end of his life, was seeking to justify his long and controversial support for her with a happy ending.

RIGHT: Frank Packenham was the 7th Earl of Longford, an Irish hereditary title created in 1785 when Ireland was still part of the United Kingdom. His son Thomas Packenham now holds, although does not use, the title.

ABOVE : Anne Morrow Lindbergh was a pioneer aviator and the first woman to receive a U.S. glider pilot license.

Anne Morrow Lindbergh, American author and aviator

(1906–2001)

The kidnap and murder of Anne and Charles Lindbergh's baby son placed an intolerable strain on their family. Her delicately expressed diaries chart her personal trauma and eventual escape from a life in the shadow of an all-American hero who fell from grace.

Anne Morrow had always wanted to marry a hero; she told her teacher as much on the night of her graduation. Charles was already famous when she first met him, for his flight across the Atlantic in *The Spirit of St Louis*. To escape the press pack which dogged his every move he took her up in his plane. They could not hear themselves above the noise of the engine and flirted with each other by written notes passed back and forth. After the pair landed, Anne wrote in her diary that 'I will never look at birds again without a leap of my heart and a keener alertness of my mind. Clouds and stars and birds: I must have been walking with head down looking at puddles for 20 years.'

The greatest test of the marriage came in 1932 with the kidnap of their first child, then aged only twenty months. Press attention focussed on Charles' heroic efforts to find the baby, largely overlooking the agony of its mother. The body of Charles Jr was found ten weeks later, and Anne was haunted by his death. 'Death to you,' she addressed herself in her diary a year later, 'is not death, nor obituary notices and quiet mourning, sermons and elegies and prayers, coffins and graves and wordy platitudes. It is not the most common experience in life - the only certainty.'

Death is the universal fate of us all, she accepted, and public rituals surrounding it are part of the shared experience of every society. However every single death is unique to those whom the departed have left behind. 'It is not what happened to Caesar and Dante and Milton and Mary Queen of Scots, to the soldiers in all the wars, to the sick in the plagues, to public men yesterday. It never happened before - what happened today to you. It has only happened to your little boy.'

Although they stayed together, Charles' and Anne's marriage buckled under the strain. The press would not let go of its obsession with the Lindberghs and hounded them and their other children until they fled to Europe to find some peace. There the couple were both impressed by the charisma of Germany's new leader Adolf Hitler; and when at length they returned to America to escape the approaching storm of war, they both urged America not to get involved. When the US did join the conflict on the side of the Allies, the Lindberghs were seen as Nazi sympathisers and their reputation was ruined. Now Anne could not even be considered "the wife of a hero."

Anne Morrow Lindbergh had always written a diary and had also published accounts of her adventures – she was the navigator and radio operator on many of her husband's ground-breaking flights. *North to the Orient* (1935), for which Antoine de Saint-Exupéry wrote a foreword, was Anne's story of their exploration of routes across the Arctic. Anne became infatuated with the Frenchman, with whom she felt connected to as a fellow writer. This was the beginning of a sense of personal validation for her, but when he disappeared during a flight in 1944, she was plunged into depression.

Anne escaped in 1947 to the island of Captiva off the Florida coast, where she found peace at last, through writing. 'I collected shells,' her diary records. 'I recognised how wonderful the freedom was of not having to do things every day and being able to go into a room and just write what one felt. ... One sees through the writing. You sink into a more authentic place inside yourself.' Following the move, her much-admired early environmental and proto-feminist novel, *Gift from the Sea*, was finished in 1953.

Frida Kahlo, Mexican painter

(1907–1954), as translated by Sarah M. Lowe

Frida Kahlo's impact on the world has been far greater since her death than it was during her short life. The woman for whom the expression "tortured soul" may well have been invented kept a journal for the final ten years of her life. This could be considered a diary with pictures, or a sketchbook with words.

Kahlo was plagued with pain and disease throughout her life. She suffered from polio at the age of seven and when she was eighteen she sustained horrific injuries in a traffic accident, the consequences of which tortured her from then on. Frida made several attempts at suicide and her death may have been the result of another. She lost several toes to gangrene, and a year before she died her right leg went the same way. Her diary from February 1954 reads, 'They amputated my leg six months ago, they have given me centuries of torture and at moments I almost lost my reason. I keep on wanting to kill myself. Diego is what keeps me from it, through my vain idea that he would miss me. ... But never in my life have I suffered more. I will wait a while ...'

Diego Rivera was Frida's husband, twice. A serial philanderer, twenty-six years older than she, he hurt her with his frequent affairs, including one with her younger sister, Cristina. Kahlo herself was no saint in matrimonial matters – her lovers included the fugitive dissident Russian revolutionary Leon Trotsky, whom Rivera had been instrumental in bringing to Mexico, and who was eventually assassinated there on Stalin's orders.

Kahlo's childhood was coloured by her parents' unhappy marriage. She was close to her father but her mother was remote. 'I am in agreement with everything my father taught me,' she told her psychologist in 1940, 'and nothing my mother taught me'. She came, through polio and other injuries, to associate pain with love, and many of her self-portraits depict her with wounds. Kahlo sought pain out, and some have suggested that she suffered from Munchhausen Syndrome, evidenced by her urge to have unnecessary surgical operations on her spine.

Frida Kahlo's diary is a remarkable artefact in which words and pictures mingle on every page, as if she were drawing on every tool at her disposal to express her thoughts. Both Frida's images and the handwriting are multi-coloured, and she used colour to express specific ideas and feelings: blue represented "electricity and purity"; yellow was for "madness, illness, fear – and happiness", Magenta was for "blood", and green for "sadness" and science. 'Nothing is black,' she wrote, 'Really nothing.'

The images drawn in the notebook are not the carefully worked art of her paintings. Nor are they preparatory sketches. There is no connection between her creative output and the drawings of her diary. The diary images were made urgently, desperately trying to communicate what words were too slow and inadequate to capture.

Her last year, after the amputation, was spent in a delirium of pain, medication, depression and more than one attempt to kill herself. In Kahlo's diary, sketches of angels and skeletons started to appear. Her final entry was a list of all the doctors and friends whom she wanted to thank for their attention to her. It closed with these words, 'I joyfully await the exit – and I hope never to return – Frida.' The final drawing was of a black angel – the Angel of Death.

RIGHT: One of the most recognisable artists of all time, Kahlo's style is characterised by Surrealism, inspired by traditional Mexican culture.

Jun Takami, Japanese author

(1907–1965)

Many wartime diaries written by Japanese participants have survived, and they provide fascinating alternative perspectives to the Pacific War sparked by the notorious attack on America's Pearl Harbor naval base. Takami Jun, a successful author before the war, kept a comprehensive journal.

Takami was born in Fukui Prefecture, the illegitimate son of the region's governor and a geisha. There is a certain sense of inevitability about his life – a description he himself used. He discovered left-wing politics at university in Tokyo and adopted the sometimes-contradictory philosophies of Humanism and Marxism. After graduation he worked for the Japanese arm of Columbia Records and wrote for leftist journals until he was arrested in 1932 as part of a clampdown on the Japanese Communist Party.

In detention, he was forced to recant his beliefs, a dubious conversion about which he wrote in the autobiographical book *Should Auld Acquaintance Be Forgot*, published in 1935. Supposed weakness of mind and confusion of thought in *Auld Acquaintance* became regular themes of his later fictional work.

Tension rose around the Pacific Ocean throughout 1941. Japan, fighting a war in China, was demanding the raising of sanctions against it by the United States and two colonial powers in the region, Britain and the Netherlands. In Japan, internal propaganda against these three nations was very successful and in November men of military service age were called up for "induction".

Takami joked with his family that, because of his prior convictions, he expected to be 'assigned to hard labour in the coal mines.' At all events, a war seemed to be coming; and when on December 2nd 1941 Japan declared war on all three countries, no one in Japan was surprised: Takami wrote in his diary, 'The inevitable has come to test our luck.' There was general support and enthusiasm for action, and even the wish that it had begun sooner.

Ironically, given the nature of his criminal record, Takami was assigned to the Investigation Bureau of the Japanese Literature Patriotic Association during the war. In the light of his job, the very existence of his diary might have been seen as a subversive act.

In it he recorded his impressions of the Japanese at home and abroad. The surprise and shock of Pearl Harbor gave Japan an early advantage; gradually however the tide turned, and so did Takami's attitude to the war. As allied bombs fell on Tokyo in 1944, he was at a railway station, trying to get his mother to safety. He wrote in his diary that what struck him most was the slow, calm manner in which everyone was going about their business. He felt a surge of affection and compatriotism for them all and realised that he wished to share their fate, whatever it might be. He wanted the war to be over, even if it meant defeat for Japan.

Takami's wartime work often took him beyond Japanese shores, and he was shocked by the Japanese Army's treatment of Chinese and Manchurian prisoners. He contrasted it with the behaviour of US troops after the Japanese surrender. 'The streets of Tokyo swarm with American servicemen,' he wrote. 'But no matter where I have gone, I have never seen an American soldier strike a Japanese or behave with an air of superiority or in a menacing manner.'

LEFT : Jun Takami was the pen-name of artist Takami Yoshio.

Joyce Grenfell, English entertainer

(1910-1979)

Wealth and high society are unlikely breeding grounds for music hall comedy. Joyce Grenfell was an English socialite with a cut-glass accent who was presented to the Queen as a debutante. She found acting to be too much like hard work, but discovered a talent for delivering comic monologues.

Joyce Grenfell was a niece of America-born Nancy Astor, Britain's first woman MP, and a granddaughter of Chiswell Phipps, an American railroad millionaire. She grew up among the monied gentry of Wiltshire in southern England and dreamt of appearing on stage – until she discovered that a lot of preparation went on before opening night. Moreover, as Grenfell realised later in her career, she had to engage with her audience, performing directly to them – facing forwards and not, as she put it, 'acting sideways'.

Her gift for comedy was discovered by a BBC producer at a dinner party in early 1939 where she was an entertaining guest. Invited to fill a spot in a forthcoming revue in an off-West-End London theatre, she stole the show and was, literally, an overnight success. Her stock-in-trade was monologues by socially gauche characters in awkward situations, exemplified by her routine about *The Old Girls' School Reunion.*

During the dark early years of World War Two, Grenfell was a regular and welcome source of laughter; and in its final years she joined ENSA, the Entertainments National Service Association, through which popular entertainers of the day toured British army bases all over the world. A habitual diarist, her wartimes journals were published posthumously as *The Time of my Life: Entertaining the Troops.*

Grenfell performed in India, the Middle East and all around the Mediterranean. She loved being centre-stage – using what she called her 'circus horse instinct'. These stages were not the ones familiar to her from her London revues. On March 25th 1944 she described one unusual setting in Naples, 'a huge surgical [ward] ... over a hundred beds in it, all in bays off a central corridor. So we did three shows, one between each bay. ... One patient, lying on his stomach, could only just see me so I had to get right into a corner so that he could peer with at least one eye!'

Some days were harder than others. It was a serious business, trying to be funny. At a field hospital in Algiers Grenfell reported, on Tuesday February 3rd 1944, that 'one of the very ill men in the first ward we did on Monday died that night. I wish I could tell his family how he smiled and even sang with us the day before he died.' That evening however, the show had to go on. 'Lots of eye patients, including a completely blinded boy who was being taken care of by a couple of pals with all the tenderness of mothers.' Grenfell was deeply moved by the compassion, in the midst of war, of men for one another.

'As if he was better invisible somehow, he kept turning up his coat collar and sinking into it. But he sang with us; and he cried a little. It was the gentleness of his two friends and their concern and solicitude that moved me so much.'

RIGHT: Joyce Grenfell, a talented stage actress from London who was also a radio critic, writer and singer.

CUNARD
LINE

ABOVE: Albert Camus, a French philosopher, who became at the age of forty-four the second-youngest recipient of the Nobel Prize for Literature in its history.

Albert Camus, Algerian-born French writer and philosopher

(1913–1960)

Born an outsider and a lifelong believer in mutual support and cooperation, the French-Algerian author rejected communism and existentialism in favour of moralism and absurdism. The comedy of life, he might have said, was a joke to be shared.

Camus had his first major success with the novel *L'Étranger*, a title which has been variously translated as *The Foreigner*, *The Outsider* or *The Stranger*. He was a *pied-noir* – a "white man with black feet", a Frenchman born in the then-French colony of Algeria. His sort was looked down on both by European Frenchmen who felt geographically superior and by Arabic Algerians who did not enjoy the same rights as the *pied-noirs*. He argued all his life for integration, whether between Arabs and Europeans in Algeria or between the many nationalities of Europe.

Central to his beliefs was Camus' early acceptance of communism, which he saw as a stepping stone toward a greater, more socio-spiritual integration of people, class and race. Camus fell out irrevocably with communism when Russia became a totalitarian state under Stalin. He maintained his opposition, however to central authority, the exploitation of human beings for profit and the ownership of property.

Camus was already a celebrated author when World War Two began, and he served with distinction in the French Resistance, emerging afterwards as something of a national hero. In the 1940s he made two lengthy visits to the Americas for lecture tours, his impressions of which are preserved in Camus' diaries.

Given his political position, one would not expect the author to be impressed with the bustling capitalist economy of New York, where he landed in March 1946. He seemed to dislike the place. 'Order, power, economic strength, they're all here. The heart trembles before so much remarkable inhumanity.' But Camus predicted that, by the evening he explained, 'I go to bed ... knowing perfectly well that I'll have changed my mind in two days.'

Sure enough, he had already begun to soften by the following morning. 'Magnificent food shops. Enough to make all of Europe burst. I admire the women in the streets, the hues of their dresses, and the colour of the taxis, which look like insects dressed in their Sunday best.'

After his first public talk, three days later, it was discovered that someone had stolen a collection box intended for the benefit of French children. 'Someone in the audience stands up to suggest everyone give the same amount on the way out that they gave on the way in. On the way out, everyone gives much more and the proceeds are considerable. Typical of American generosity. Their hospitality and cordiality are also like this, immediate and without affectation. This is what's best about them.' Camus' American diaries are a delight of such discoveries and descriptions of their generosity.

Carolina Maria de Jesus, Brazilian writer and social activist

(1914–1977)

The *favelas*, the ghettos of São Paolo, drained the humanity from their inhabitants, whose lives were dominated entirely by poverty and hunger. One slum-dweller dreamed of a better life; Carolina de Jesus kept a diary on found scraps of paper as a record of her imagination and her reality.

Carolina was the daughter of a single woman and a married man in a rural inland Brazilian town. An outcast from birth thanks to her illegitimacy, she attended school just long enough to learn to read and write, something her mother had never done. Carolina's mother died in 1937 when she was twenty-three and Carolina made her way to Sao Paolo, then a rapidly expanding city.

There was plenty of work for a Black woman willing to be a live-in maid to rich White Brazilians, but Carolina's unwillingness to accept this position made it hard for her to hold down a job. When she became pregnant in 1947, she found herself homeless in the *Canindé favela* of the city where, like many others she built herself a shack from found materials. Carolina lived from hand to mouth, collecting and selling recyclable rubbish to pay for food for herself and, over time, her three children by three different men.

Carolina was regarded with suspicion by the illiterate *favelados* among whom she lived. Reading and writing suggested to them that she was a witch incanting spells. For her part she looked down on them for their unwillingness to better themselves; 'The women point out that I'm not married. But I'm happier than all of them.' She wrote of a community where alcoholism and domestic violence were rife. 'At night, while the women cry for help, I calmly listen to Viennese waltzes in my shack. While the husbands break down the shack planks, my kids and I sleep soundly. I don't envy the married women of the *favela* that live their lives like slaves.'

She was angry with the *favelados* for accepting the idea that the colour of their skin made them inferior. 'I adore my black skin and my kinky hair. The Negro hair is more educated than the white man's hair. Because with Negro hair, where you put it, it stays. It's obedient. The hair of the white, just give one quick movement, and it's out of place. It won't obey. If reincarnation exists I want to come back black.'

Carolina's diary is a valuable historic record of conditions in the slums, some of which still exist today. She railed against the patronising weasel words of politicians and priests in their response to the squalor. Of one visiting monk who preached acceptance of her lot, she wrote that if he 'saw his children eating rotten food already attacked by vultures and rats, . . . [he] would rebel, because rebellion comes from bitterness.' As for state officials, 'Those who govern our country are those who have money, who don't know what hunger is, or pain or poverty.'

The tone of Carolina's writing becomes more world-weary during the course of her diary, although she never gave up the possibility of a better life. 'I dreamt I was an angel,' she once wrote. 'My dress was billowing and had long pink sleeves. I went from earth to heaven. I put stars in my hands and played with them. I talked to the stars. They put on a show in my honor. They danced around me and made a luminous path. When I woke up I thought: I'm so poor. I can't afford to go to a play so God sends me these dreams for my aching soul.' Carolina's evocative description of her dreams is a powerful argument for education. How many poets are lost to the world because they cannot read and write?

ABOVE : Carolina Maria de Jesus, a memorialist whose offers an eye-opening account of her experiences in the Brazilian favelas.

ABOVE : Alec Guinness, the British actor who is today remembered for his performances as Fagin in Oliver Twist, *Obi Wan Kenobi in* Star Wars, *and - twice - as* Hamlet *(in 1938 and 1951).*

Sir Alec Guinness, English actor

(1914–2000)

One of the great British actors of the twentieth century, Sir Alec Guinness was known to older generations for his Ealing comedies, and to younger ones for his role in the original *Star Wars* trilogy as Obi Wan Kenobi. His diaries combine a mischievous humour with the occasional settling of scores.

There has always been a mixture of over-demonstrative affection and backstage cattiness among theatre people, or "luvvies" as they sometimes like to think of themselves. This affection comes from the transient lives which actors live, working intensely with each other for a few weeks of rehearsal and performance, before all going their separate ways to other plays in other theatres. The cattiness arises because every actor is a performer and may prefer to be the centre of attention, rather than an extra in someone else's drama.

Alec Guinness and Lawrence Olivier were born only seven years apart and their careers crossed paths on many occasions. Guinness claimed that Olivier tried to sabotage the career of many rival actors, and would have done so to Guinness's 'if he'd had the chance.' The two first met in 1935, working on a production of *Romeo and Juliet* in which Guinness played the apothecary and Gielgud and Olivier swapped roles as Mercutio and Romeo. Of Olivier, Guinness had mixed feelings. He wrote that 'we all thought he looked and behaved like the leader of a dance band. But his Romeo was as arresting and beautiful as his Mercutio was vulgar and gimmicky.'

Reviewers thought that Gielgud's Romeo was the more romantic of the two, and Guinness admitted that 'many of us were ... too admiring of John to value Larry's qualities fairly.' Of Olivier, Guinness thought that 'there was a touch of pretension about him, and his public speeches were fulsome and awful.'

The day after Olivier's death in 1989, Alec Guinness reflected on the man at length in his diary. He recalled some great and not-so-great performances. 'His "I defy you, stars'" in Romeo was memorable. And so was his "Poor naked wretches etc" in *Lear*. But his famous howl in *Oedipus* I thought just tiresome.' It's the howl that was parodied to hilarious effect by Derek Jacobi, playing the part of a once-great actor in an episode of the US sit-com *Frasier*.

'He knew every trick of the trade,' Guinness commented, 'I'm not sure he was an artist but he was total actor - a giant among actors.'

He did not reserve his critical asides for Olivier only. Following a spate of celebrity deaths around Christmas 1994, he remarked that 'Death has [taken] John Osborne, Fanny Cradock and Peter Cook ... all regrettable, but the theatre did not begin with [Osborne's masterpiece] Look Back in Anger, Cradock's cookery appeared to me over-elaborate and ill-tempered, and Peter Cook's obituaries took up more press coverage than would the assassination of the Royal Family.'

Guinness had a theatrical skill in delivering a succinct "bitchy" barb, and when the actor John Mills gave the eulogy at John Gielgud's funeral (three months before Guiness's own), Alec commented in his diary, 'Johnnie Mills – a tiny white bearded gnome – spoke about himself.'

Nina Sergeyevna Lugovskaya, Russian teenager

(1918-1993)

The diary of a young Russian woman who suffered at the hands of a brutal regime has often been compared to that of Anne Frank. The outcomes for the two girls were very different, and through her obsessions with "pessimism and boys" Nina Lugovskaya comes over as the more archetypal teenager.

Nina Lugovskaya began to keep a diary at the age of thirteen. When she was nineteen it was confiscated during a raid on the family home by Stalin's secret police, the NKVD (*Narodnyy Komissariat Vnutrennikh Del*, translated as "the People's Commissariat for Internal Affairs"). The outpourings of her unhappy teenage heart were seized on by the NKVD as evidence of dissidence and non-conformity, and the diary was used to incriminate Nina, her two sisters and her parents, who consequently served prison terms in the gulags of the Kolyma peninsula east of Siberia.

All of them survived and went on to live productive lives. Nina settled in the east, married a fellow inmate and had a successful career as an artist and theatre designer. After her death, and after the fall of the Soviet Union, researchers found among the family's NKVD the diary itself, undamaged apart from the frequent underlining by NKVD investigators of suspicious passages. Like all teenagers she was anti-authoritarian, and suspicion can only have been aroused by diary entries such as this: 'We all want to annoy [the teachers], to play dirty tricks, and then refuse to say who did it rather than betray a friend (that is what earns our respect). ... We don't have the new, good attitude – what they now call the "Soviet attitude".' The Bolsheviks, it seemed, were to blame for everything. 'Homework, my God, we have so much homework,' she complained. 'What wretches the Bolsheviks are! They don't think about us at all, don't think that we're people too.'

Sometimes she became dangerously specific in her complaints. Once she reported a dream in which she tried to kill Stalin, 'the vile Georgian who is crippling Russia.' She applauded a real-life assassination attempt on the Soviet leader and had no time for the politically correct "Soviet attitude" which was spoon-fed to them at school. 'To hell with the new society!,' she erupted with naïve fury. One wonders how Gennady's life turned out.

Nina's political language and ideas undoubtedly came from her greatly loved father: 'he's a revolutionary ... a man of ideas, a man of action, a man who sticks steadfastly to his views and won't trade them for anything in the world.' He was a member of the Socialist Revolutionary Party which was idealistically opposed to the Bolsheviks, and before Nina's incriminating diary came to light he had already been exiled on three previous occasions.

Nina recalled his arrest of 1932 in her diary. 'Today they herded us out to march around the streets, which made me absolutely furious .... Walking over the cold, gray ground in the damp, dull light of an autumn day ... and cursing Soviet power to myself.' Nina became more aware of her language as time went on, and the opposite sex became more of a focus than the Bolsheviks. 'What if the apartment is suddenly searched and it is confiscated because of my completely uncensored remarks about Stalin? And it winds up in the hands of the secret police? They'll read it and laugh at my amorous gibberish.' Nina would grow up to learn about the true nature of Soviet society. And to discover that no one laughed at the NKVD.

ABOVE: *A 1930s Moscow school, similar to the one Nina would have attended. Nina is remembered for her writing and her oil paintings, which are still exhibited today.*

Hélène Berr, French observer of the Nazi occupation of Paris

(1921–1945), as translated by David Bellos

There are myriad heartbreaking diaries of lives cut short by Nazi Germany's efforts to exterminate the Jews. Sometimes it's easier to think of only one – Anne Frank's – rather than to imagine thousands. However, each account records a life worth living, and represents a death worth noting.

Hélène Berr's diary was kept for three years during the German occupation of Paris. Its final entry, on February 15th 1944, reads simply, 'Horror, horror, horror.' Hélène was quoting a line from Shakespeare's *Macbeth*, at the moment when Macduff discovers the murder of the gentle King Duncan.

Berr had just learned from a released prisoner of the fate which, unknown to her, would be her own. He described the burial pits into which the dead and dying were thrown. 'Typhus took hold,' he had told her, 'and hundreds dropped dead each day. Each morning the Germans went round with guns finishing off those who were no longer able to stand up.'

Hélène Berr was a bright, lively student, studying English Literature at the Sorbonne. During the course of the diary her entries record the progress of her thesis, which she continued to work on even after Jewish people were forbidden from graduating, such was her enthusiasm for what she described as the 'selfish magic' of her subject.

Hélène played the violin, in an age when musical accomplishment was expected of young women; and she was called upon to give informal recitals. 'Here we had tea on the small table, listening to the "Kreutzer" sonata,' she wrote of one such afternoon on August 11th 1942. 'He sat at the piano without being asked and played some Chopin. Afterward, I played the violin.' 'He' was Jean Morawiecki, her new boyfriend, to whom she would entrust the pages of her diary and from whom, remarkably, they were recovered intact in 1994.

Hélène's diary records the innocent delights of daily life from start to finish; but it diverged over the course of its three years, becoming also a parallel journal of the reality of being a Jew in German Paris. The two collide in an entry from June 4th 1942, after the Nazis had begun to require that all Jewish people identify themselves by wearing a yellow star. 'I want to stay very elegant and dignified at all times so that people can see what that means. I want to do whatever is most courageous. This evening I believe that means wearing the star.'

Later that year her father was arrested for not wearing his star properly. Her mother had attached it with snaps so that it could be transferred from one jacket to another without unpicking the threads and re-sewing it every time. From his prison camp he managed somehow to send a note to her mother, describing conditions. 'I couldn't really make out Papa's note because Maman was sobbing so hard that it stopped me concentrating,' she noted on September 20th 1942. 'For the time being I couldn't cry. But if misfortune does come, I shall be sorrowful enough, sorrowful for all time.'

The family were all eventually sent to Auschwitz, where both her parents died. Hélène was sent on the so-called "Death March" to Bergen-Belsen concentration camp. There she contracted typhus, was beaten senseless by a guard when she was too weak to appear for roll-call, and died either then or some time after as a result of the injuries to her already depleted body. The camp was liberated only five days later. Hélène was twenty-four.

LEFT: In June 1940 the Nazi swastika flies on a flag on the Arc de Triomphe, in German-occupied Paris.

Ina Konstantinova, Soviet World War II partisan

(1924–1944)

Germany and the Soviet Union signed a non-aggression pact on the eve of World War Two, which agreed the division of the countries between them in the event of war. Less than two years later, after several breaches of the pact on both sides, Hitler launched a full-scale invasion of the USSR.

Germany's campaign against the Soviet Union was arguably Hitler's biggest tactical mistake. Russia was able to mobilise its resources and population effectively, portraying the attack as an assault on the very survival of the country by calling it "The Great Patriotic War". The conflict took a terrible toll on both sides but ultimately the German Army was repelled and the Soviets lent their considerable resources to the Allies for the remainder of the war.

Ina Konstantinova had always kept a diary, and as she turned sixteen in 1940, she was reflective and mature about her great age. 'On the last day of my childhood,' she wrote on July 29th, 'it is painful to give up all that is close and dear to us, especially one's childhood. I know one thing: the pure, radiant joys of childhood are gone forever.' The Soviet Union was already at war, having just invaded Finland; and Ina could have been speaking for all the children of Europe when she wrote: 'Good-bye, my morning. My day, bright but exhausting, has begun. And there, at the end, my old age awaits me. But will I reach it?'

Ina lived in the west of the Soviet Union, near the border with Poland which was the point of entry for many of the German forces on June 22nd 1941. She was a dutiful member of the Komsomol, the Soviet youth movement which indoctrinated citizens with communist ideology from an early age. Too young to fight, she volunteered for, or was assigned, duties with the Red Cross, treating wounded Russian soldiers and partisans. Only a few days later, on July 3rd, her diary recounted the injuries which she was required to patch up in one particularly arduous all-night shift. Ina wrote, 'I could never fully describe what I lived through that night. I was completely tired out. But it didn't matter!'

She sounds exhausted but also filled with exhilaration to be serving her country. Ina's mood changed however when, at just over seventeen, she was given the news that her boyfriend had been killed in the fighting. After this she ran away from home to join the partisans in Moscow. 'My dear ones, please forgive me!,' she journalled in July 1942. 'I know – it was mean on my part to treat you as I did, but it's better this way: under no circumstances could I have withstood Mama's tears. Don't be too upset, don't feel sorry for me, because my fondest, long-standing wish has come true. I am happy!'

Ina threw herself into work, often behind enemy lines, acting as a forward observer to report enemy advances. 'At night a large punitive detachment approached our village very, very close', she reported on June 19th 1943. 'The exchange of fire continued throughout the night. ... Soon the first casualty was brought to me. My hands were covered with blood, then took this seriously wounded man to a doctor, 6 kms away. When I returned, we had to execute a certain village elder, a collaborator. We went to get him; we read him the sentence and led him to the pace of execution. I felt awful.'

In time Ina Konstantinova was trained in the use of a machine gun. She was giving covering fire for her retreating unit on March 4th 1944 when she was killed by a German bullet. Ina died at twenty, having never reached the old age which she imagined as a sixteen-year-old.

RIGHT: Many women, such as Ina and the Soviet ambulance woman seen here, were a part of the fighting effort on both sides of the war.

LEFT: Tony Benn, seen here in Brighton in 1989, attending the Labour Party conference.

Tony Benn, English Socialist politician

(1925-2014)

Tony Benn was a giant of the British political scene. He served in parliament for fifty years and then retired 'in order to spend more time on politics.' Staunchly socialist in his outlook, Benn renounced his inherited peerage in order to remain an MP. He published nine volumes of diaries.

Anthony Wedgwood Benn, the former Viscount Stansgate, was for many years considered to be a moderate amongst the ranks of Britain's left-wing Labour Party. Reflecting in later life on the far-left Militant group within the party, he commented, 'On the one hand, you have got all these people who are simply concerned with power; and on the other, you've got sectarians who are simply concerned with ideological purity; and somewhere in the middle somebody has to try ... to bring it all together for the good of the people we represent.'

As British politics drifted to the right however in the 1960s and 1970s, he became increasingly isolated both inside and outside his party, vilified by the press and at best ignored by his colleagues as a relic of Labour's past. When Margaret Thatcher's Conservative Party was elected Benn was mindful of the significance. '4 May 1979 - a dramatic day in British politics. The most right-wing Conservative Government and Leader for fifty years; the first woman Prime Minister. I cannot absorb it all.' Still, Benn relished the prospect of the fight ahead, released from the necessary compromises of loyalty when Labour were in power. 'I have the freedom now to speak my mind, and this is probably the beginning of the most creative period of my life. I am one of the few ex-Ministers who enjoys Opposition and I intend to take full advantage of it.'

Benn was a thorn in the side of politicians of every stripe from then on, and a gulf opened between him and his former colleagues as they tried to move in on Thatcher's ground. Of the next Labour leader, once a political ally of Benn's, he wrote, 'Michael Foot is hopeless.' Foot's successor had already struck Benn as 'not a substantial person ... a media figure really' in 1976; and when Neil Kinnock lost the election in 1992, Benn declared that he had destroyed Labour 'financially, as well as politically, morally and intellectually and organisationally.'

Benn was in general kinder to his enemies than to his political friends. Tony Benn considered Norman Tebbit, Thatcher's staunchest ally in the disempowerment of the trade unions, 'terribly soft and good-natured ... really a rather decent guy.' He admired Enoch Powell, who stirred up racial divisions, for 'his sheer ability and lucidity [which] would carry him upward;' and as Labour moved ever further to the right of centre, Benn wrote in 1994 that 'I remind myself of Enoch Powell in his latter days.'

Ian Paisley, the Northern Irish opponent of the reunification of Ireland, was described as 'a very nice guy ... [with] a good class sense ... an amusing guy.' Benn reflected in 2008 that Paisley 'has openly and honestly argued in favour of what he believed to be the interests of those he represented. ... In politics, I think you have to say what you mean and mean what you say, and I think Ian did that.' Even Margaret Thatcher, who began the dismantling of so much of the state apparatus in which Tony Benn believed, earned his respect for her adherence to her own principles. On the day that she lost the leadership of her party, November 22nd 1990, 'we had the censure debate. ... Thatcher was brilliant. She always has her ideology to fall back on; she rolled off statistics, looked happy and joked.'

Allen Ginsberg, American beat poet

(1926–1997)

The son of a poet (his father) and a Marxist (his mother), Allen Ginsberg formed – with Jack Kerouac and William S Burroughs – the core of the Beat Generation of the 1950s and 1960s. He kept diaries throughout his life, in which he recorded both his inner and outer journeys.

Beat poetry was a heady mix of sex, drugs and jazz inspired by notions of personal freedom which were themselves rooted in the works of Ralph Waldo Emerson, Henry David Thoreau, Walt Whitman and other writers. In turn, the beatniks of Ginsberg's generation paved the way for the liberated "sex, drugs and rock'n'roll" of 1960s hippy culture, followed by the reactionary anarchy of the punk generation.

Ginsberg and other leading figures of beat poetry first converged on the campus of Columbia University, where Ginsberg and Kerouac were both students in 1944. Ginsberg's breakthrough came with a public reading in San Francisco of his poem *Howl*, rich in explicit descriptions of sex, which became the subject on an obscenity trial.

He travelled extensively and always kept a journal, in which Ginsberg recorded his dreams and waking state of mind, as well as the places and people which he encountered, often in undecipherable streams of consciousness. In Paris, he made an apartment above a bar his base for several years, which became known as "the Beat Hotel" because of the many poets who visited him there.

In one sequence of diary entries from 1961 he returns to a dream which he had noted on March 23rd during a crossing to Europe from America. 'Dream of long worm in my breast crawling to my neck, serrations rippling on the skin – I pluck it out part thru a raw gooey hole – only get segments – Peter [Orlovsky, Ginsberg's life partner] presses knife to my skin & cuts off the tail.' The snake appears to have been a phallic symbol.

Back in "the Beat Hotel" on April 9th, Ginsberg was in a gloomy mood: 'What's left? Nothing but this body with reproductive organs. ... What can we apprehend but our own emptiness? That we exist ... What for? to reproduce ourselves? ... The trial of existence is a complete failure. To have entered heroin in my body and lie in Paris bed in black bathrobe with thoughts flitting thru my reproductive organs.' Ginsberg, then thirty-four years old, had begun taking drugs many years earlier in an attempt to recreate the hallucinatory visions he had experienced in 1948 while reading passages of William Blake's poetry.

Later the same day, as the heroin took over, he returned to his thoughts. 'The great snake from 0000 to 1961 which many have entered & left, streams forward inching on itself thru a million eyes – does this great being want to continue with me? Do I even like this snake that for all I know will only end up chewing its own tail? I who masturbate and will die? Can it do better than masturbate?'

Kerouac and Burroughs were constant presences in Ginsberg's diaries and frequently in his dreams. During an outing from Paris to Tangiers in 1961 he described one. 'Dream: June 15, 1961. Jack [Kerouac], Bill [Burroughs],Gregory [Corso, another poet] & self are gathered in Egypt to confer over the future of the Mystery Cosmos-we decide that "To Be or Not to Be" is the question ... the Choice come to climax before us is whether or not really to continue the experiment of life in this or any form.' From this he woke 'in anxiety to get my warning listened to. "the last best hope on earth-the bourgeois mob" – Arrest death!' For all his existential, drug-induced angst, Ginsberg decided to live to the age of seventy, providing and inspiring a link between the Beat Generation and its successor the Hippy Movement.

ABOVE: Allen Ginsberg was a performer as well as a poet, and recordings of his distinctive voice still survive. Many scholars and schoolchildren study his works today, most notably Howl.

Che Guevara, Argentine revolutionary

(1928–1967), as translated by The Che Guevara Studies Center

Ernesto "Che" Guevara was an Argentine doctor who saw such poverty and oppression during his travels in South America that he became convinced of the need for revolution. He was a prolific writer who prepared his own diaries for publication and wrote a handbook of guerrilla warfare.

Guevara was an avid reader of world literature and philosophy, whom the CIA once patronisingly characterised as 'fairly intellectual for a Latino'. He believed in education as a force for change and encouraged his troops to teach local peasants to read and write. Che himself used to read to his men from the works of Miguel de Cervantes, Robert Louis Stevenson and others.

Although he intended to serve the cause of revolution in a medical capacity, he trained alongside soldiers and proved to be an instinctively brilliant guerrilla fighter. He first saw revolutionary action in Guatemala, where he and his comrades failed to prevent the CIA-backed overthrow of a socialist government. In Cuba, during the struggle to overthrow Fulgencio Batista, even his enemies admired his grasp of military strategy. Che became Fidel Castro's right-hand man after the revolution.

In the 1960s however, he became convinced that his true calling was in fomenting new revolutions rather than managing old ones. After an unsuccessful spell in strife-torn Congo, he turned his attention back to South America, and to Bolivia, with the aim of overthrowing the country's military government. From the outset his campaign there was beset with difficulties. There were divisions between the Cuban and Bolivian factions of his guerrilla force which undermined the mutual loyalty which Guevara believed essential to an efficient unit. The terrain in the shadow of the Andes was unfamiliar, progress slow and his maps inaccurate. Very early on in the campaign the guerillas lost communication with Cuba because their radios rusted in the humid climate.

LEFT: Che Guevara's image has become famous around the world. A symbol of revolution he has been memorialised in artworks, film, and television.

Guevara underestimated the charisma and popularity of the Bolivian president; and above all he overestimated the appetite of the Bolivian peasantry for revolution. For example, on April 16th 1966, they arrived at a small hamlet called Bella Vista. 'This is a settlement of four peasants, who sold us potatoes, a pig, and some corn. They are poor peasants and are very frightened by our presence here.' Living in such poverty, the peasants chose readily available money over future revolution. 'Talking to these peasants is like talking to statues,' he complained. 'They do not give us any help. Worse still, many of them are turning into informants.'

Frustrated, he took to holding peasants hostage as he moved from one area to another. 'We remained in the area the entire day,' he wrote on April 19th, 'detaining peasants coming from both directions, so that we obtained a wide assortment of prisoners.' He learned that his presence had already been discovered. One of the peasants 'confessed that his brother and a farmhand ... had gone to collect the reward of 500 to 1,000 pesos. We confiscated a horse from him as a reprisal, and made this known to the peasants being held.' It was in every sense an uphill struggle.

The attempt in Bolivia was to be his last campaign. Once again the CIA and other US military units worked with the Bolivian Army to contain his revolutionary activities. He was captured on March 8th 1967 and executed the following day to avoid the publicity of a show trial. Guevara's Bolivian diary was found among his effects.

Andy Warhol, American artist

(1928–1987)

Andy Warhol completed his most famous works during the 1960s. From the 1970s he began to capitalise on his success both socially and commercially, mingling with the rich and famous and charging $25,000 to paint a portrait. His diary is a "Who's Who" of twentieth-century celebrity.

Warhol's attitude to his art changed following an attempt on his life in The Factory in 1968. The Factory was his studio and a meeting point for other artists and to host their outrageous 1960s parties. His would-be assassin was Valerie Solanas, an extreme feminist who believed that Warhol was intending to steal her work and that all men should be eliminated. Warhol nearly died and his injuries plagued him for the rest of his life. Afterwards he took greater control of The Factory and of the business side of his art. The Factory became more an office than a nightclub.

Warhol's output from then on, with some notable exceptions, showed a loss of depth and innovation. He traded on his trademark screen-printing technique and once-radical bright colours, and took on projects on the basis that 'they would sell.' On one occasion he painted twelve variations of the same portrait for the actress Pia Zadora – she bought two of them and they were unveiled at a party to which press photographers were invited. As Warhol recalled in his diary on September 6th 1983, with apparent amusement, 'one of the photographers said, "How could Andy Warhol sink to such mediocrity?" and the photographer he said it to said, "What do you mean? He's famous for sinking to mediocrity."'

One of Warhol's diary quirks was a need to record the price of the taxis he took to the glamorous parties he attended. 'Cabbed to Clemente's ($5),' he wrote on February 10th 1987. 'Robert Mapplethorpe was there. He looked more healthy than I've ever seen him, he had color in his face.' Mapplethorpe's art was his striking photography of the male form. He was battling with complications from HIV/AIDs, from which he would die two years after Warhol. 'I think they're trying out a new drug on him, I hope he makes it.'

Warhol often referred to his shooting and saw his life divided into before and after the moment he was struck. Robert F Kennedy was shot the day after he was, and so he was always reminded of the time. For instance, 'Robert Kennedy, Jr. was on TV for the tenth anniversary of when his father was shot,' he noted on June 2nd 1978, 'so it's ten years since I was shot, too—he was the day after me.'

Shootings in the news, or on the streets of New York, always affected him. On December 8th 1980 he was attending a gala dinner at the Met Museum when 'Someone who came in said John Lennon was shot and no one could believe it, so someone called the Daily News and they said it was true. It was scary, it was all anyone could talk about. He was shot outside his house.' Warhol was a friend of the former Beatles guitarist and his wife Yoko Ono, and showed the couple round New York when they first arrived in the city in 1971.

A few months later another shooting made the headlines. Warhol was at lunch on May 13th 1981 and 'everybody was gathered around the TV and the pope had been shot. I started screaming, I got so mad —"We lost a portrait that day when Reagan was shot and I don't want it to happen again! Turn that TV off!"' Later that evening, he recorded: 'Went to Halston's and Liza Minnelli was there. They had a copy of the Post there that had "POPE SHOT" in red. It was great.' One assumes that it was the glamorous company or the newspaper's red headline that impressed the artist, and not the shooting of Pope John Paul II. Andy Warhol was a devout Byzantine Catholic.

ABOVE: Andy Warhol is perhaps the most famous figure in the pop art movement. His works are exhibited around the world today.

ABOVE: After Anne Frank's death in 1945, her diary was given to her father, the only member of the family to survive the war.

Anne Frank, Dutch Holocaust victim

(1929-1945), as translated by Barbara Mooyaart-Doubleday

The most famous diary in the world contains two years of the life of a young girl whose future, like so many others, was cut short by Nazi Germany's determination to exterminate the Jewish people.

Anne Frank was born in Frankfurt but raised in Amsterdam, where her family had fled in 1934 after the rise of Nazism in Germany. She wrote her first diary pages in a notebook which she was given for her thirteenth birthday on June 12th 1942. 'I hope I will be able to confide everything to you, as I have never been able to confide in anyone, and I hope you will be a great source of comfort and support,' her entry that day reads.

Restrictions on Jewish people were already in place, which Anne recorded on June 20th. 'Jews were required to wear a star; Jews were required to turn in their bicycles; Jews were forbidden to use trams; Jews were forbidden to ride in cars, even their own; Jews were required to do their shopping between 3.00 and 5.00pm; Jews were required to frequent only Jewish-owned barber shops and beauty salons; Jews were forbidden to be out on the streets between 8.00pm and 6.00am; Jews were forbidden to go to theatres, cinemas or any other forms of entertainment; ... Jews were forbidden to go rowing; Jews were forbidden to take part in any athletic activity in public; ... Jews were required to attend Jewish schools, etc. You couldn't do this and you couldn't do that, but life went on.'

Once deportations began however, the family went into hiding, on July 6th, in secret rooms contained within a closed annex of her father's business premises. They remained there, helped by sympathetic friends and undetected for two years, and critical ones in the personal development of a teenage girl. Anne's diaries bear witness to her growing pains – her hopes for the future, her romantic feelings, her exploration of her own body, her first rude jokes, and the growing wisdom of her diary entries.

She had ambitions to become a writer, which were encouraged when she heard a broadcast from London in March 1944 by an exiled member of the Dutch government appealing for people to keep diaries and letters for a future archive of the nation's suffering. The tide of war was turning against Germany and the family had hopes of being able to emerge soon from hiding.

Anne began to revise her diary in May that year for the benefit of that archive. She rewrote some entries and omitted others of no interest or in which she had made cruel remarks to friends or family. 'I wouldn't be able to write that kind of thing anymore,' she commented of an earlier passage. 'Now that I'm rereading my diary after a year and a half, I'm surprised at my childish innocence. Deep down I know I could never be that innocent again, however much I'd like to be.' Hence there are two different *Anne Frank's Diaries* and the contrast between the two further illustrates her growth.

Anne's last diary entry on August 1st 1944 is a heartbreaking consideration of her emergent grown-up-self versus the flippant child she has been. 'I'm afraid that people who know me as I usually am will discover I have another side, a better and finer side. I'm afraid they'll mock me, think I'm ridiculous and sentimental and not take me seriously. ... I keep trying to find a way to become what I'd like to be and what I could be if ... there were no other people in the world.' The family's hiding place was discovered on August 4th.

Jahanara Imam, Bangladeshi Freedom fighter

(1929-1994), as translated by Mustafizur Rahman

One woman, born in British Bengal, lived to see not only the independence of India and its partition but the emergence of an independent Bengali state, Bangladesh. Her diaries describe the brutal war which won that independence, at the cost of her own son and her husband.

When Britain began to accept that it must relinquish its imperial hold on India, it sought to minimise religious strife in the vast sub-continent by creating, in 1947, separate states: one for Hindus and Sikhs (India) and another for Muslims (Pakistan). Muslims constituted large majorities in both the far eastern and the far western parts of the country, and so Pakistan was a nation of two quite separate halves.

As 6.5 million Indian-Muslims rushed to Pakistan and 4.7 million Pakistani-Hindus raced to India, violence erupted between two countries who were now defined by their religion. This, the was largest mass migration in human history. Pakistan's ruling power base was in West Pakistan, and Bengalis in East Pakistan began to agitate for self-determination in their part of the country. The movement was brutally suppressed in 1971 by a campaign of genocide by West Pakistan's military government of Hindu Bengali. A Bengali guerrilla army coalesced and was joined by India – already involved in a border dispute with West Pakistan over the region of Kashmir, which continues to this day. By the end of the year, Pakistan had been defeated and in 1972 the United Nations recognised Bangladesh as a separate sovereign state.

On Pakistan's annual National Day, March 23rd 1971, Jahanara Imam joined others demanding a Bengali Free State and chanting "Joy Bangla" – "Long Live Bengal," as she wrote in her diary. 'Today is the day of resistance. Early in the morning, all of us in the house went to the rooftop and raised the new flag of independent Bangladesh next to the black flag. I felt a tickling in my chest.'

The Bangladesh genocide began two days later. 'In the morning,' Jahanara reported, 'the sound of gunfire paused for a while. ... Rumi and I set out in the car. ... When we reached the vegetable sellers' area of New Market, Rumi hit the brakes with "Oh God"! The entire market was gutted by fire. Parts of it still smoldering. I screamed, "Look, there are charred human bodies too." Rumi said, "Amma, don't look."'

Rumi, her eldest son, wanted to join the guerrilla forces but Jahanara refused. As Pakistani atrocities mounted, however, Rumi pleaded that he did not want to have to admit for the rest of his life that he did nothing. In the end, 'I shut my eyes tightly,' his mother wrote on April 21st, 'and said, "Alright, I concede. I sacrifice you to the country. Go, enrol in the war."'

One night, a Pakistani army officer came to her house and took away Rumi, her younger son Jami and her husband Sharif. Jami and Sharif were released after they had been tortured yet Sharif subsequently suffered a heart attack and, because power had been cut by the fighting, he could not be resuscitated. Rumi was never seen again. Jahanara Imam's diary of the war became a founding testament to the new Bangladeshi nation, and she spent the rest of her life campaigning for justice for Pakistani war crimes. Rumi's killer was found, convicted and executed in 2015.

RIGHT : A mural of Jahanara Imam is seen as the backdrop to the 2013 Shahbag protests in Bangladesh's capital, Dhaka.

এই আন্দোলনকে এখনো দুস্তর পথ পাড়ি দিতে হবে
আমি জানি জনগনের মত বিশ্বস্ত কেউ নয়
জয় আমাদের হবেই...

Hervé Guibert, French writer and AIDS activist

(1955–1991), as translated by Clara Orban and Todd Meyers

Cytomegalovirus is usually a harmless illness, many of us may have had it and not even have known. But for those with a lowered immune system, such as HIV/AIDS patients, its effects can be devastating. One patient kept a diary of his hospitalisation with it, in which he confronted his own mortality.

Hervé Guibert was already a celebrated French novelist when he contracted AIDS in 1988. AIDS was first identified in 1981, predominantly in drug users and gay men. Owing to the fact it occurred among these marginalised groups of society, already ostracised by many, attitudes to those suffering from complications of the syndrome were often unsympathetic. In any case, the condition was not understood and effective treatment of it unknown.

When Guibert was admitted to a Paris hospital in the autumn of 1991, he was met with ignorance, poor medical practice and disrespect. He kept a diary of his three weeks of treatment, partly as a way of punctuating the long days, of giving 'rhythm to time', and partly as a means of 'preserving my humanity.'

Guibert began his journal on September 17th 1991. 'Vision in my right eye is shot: difficulty reading. Listen to music: not yet deaf.' Cytomegalovirus attacked the eyes. The next day his condition was confirmed by an ultrasound scan. 'Cytomegalovirus! Hospitalization. Lenses right on the retina. I'm afraid they'll make me sleep in paper sheets, under a synthetic blanket. The will to live – marvellous or sickening?'

Medical staff perceived him only as a patient with an unpopular and terminal disease, while Guibert was determined to see himself as an entire human being. This inequality of perception contributed to the lack of respect he experienced. One example was the provision of only one spoon, with which he was expected to eat both his soup and his dessert at mealtimes; seemingly trivial, it was symptomatic of his being treated as different and lesser. The standard of hygiene in Guibert's ward was poor, despite the greater risk of infection from his compromised immunity.

The more Guibert observed this attitude, the more he fought it. When he was expected to wear an all-revealing transparent gown during surgery, he refused. Where was his dignity, his modesty? '"The only way you'll get me to accept it", he wrote of his conversation with a nurse, "would be to accompany me, in the same outfit, and I'll authorize you to keep your bra, just as you authorize me to keep my underwear."'

'You have to make them respect you,' he wrote. Following his diagnosis of AIDS, Guibert wrote three semi-autobiographical novels which confronted the stigma attached to the disease and remain important documents of the period. He was determined to express the impact of it on his generation and to bring it into the light, out of the supposedly murky world of "junkies and gays". Writing became Guibert's protective screen against the illness, and death.

After three weeks in the hospital he was sent home and wrote his final entry. He could no longer see well enough to continue. 'Writing in the dark? Writing until the end? Putting an end to it so as not to end up fearing death?' He attempted suicide and died two weeks later from the complications of the attempt.

LEFT : Guibert seen in Paris, France in 1988.
Around 30,000 people died of AIDS-related causes in France, during the period between 1983 and 1995.

Kurt Cobain, American rock musician

(1967-1994)

Kurt Cobain's suicide earned him membership of the so-called "27 Club", a tragic list of musicians who have died at that age. Like many of its members, Cobain struggled with the trappings of success in popular music and his chaotic journals are evidence of a troubled mind.

Kurt Cobain's widow, Courtney Love took the decision to publish his diaries and letters in 2002, and their daughter Frances, who was only twenty months old when he died, has said that she will never read them. Many published diaries are edited to preserve the privacy or embarrassment of living people and Frances' reaction raises questions about the ethics of making private writings publicly available. When Cobain wrote, 'Please read my diary, look through my things and figure me out,' was he inviting the whole world, or just his wife?

Cobain's diaries are made even more intimate by being reproduced as facsimiles, not simply transcriptions. The condition of his handwriting is as communicative as his words, and his meaning is often amplified by drawings – for example on the first page where his use of the phrase 'we were this close [to visiting a friend]' is accompanied by a sketch of his thumb and forefinger showing just how close.

Kurt Cobain was the frontman for Nirvana, a grunge band from the northwestern United States. In his journals, he explains the choice of the band's name: 'Nirvana means freedom from pain and suffering in the external world and that's close to my definition of punk rock.' He brought to the band all the iconoclastic anti-authoritarian attitudes of punk – which, come to think of it, are the iconoclastic anti-authoritarian attitudes of the young in every generation. 'Art is sacred,' he writes. 'Punk rock is freedom. Expression and right to express is vital. Anyone can be artistic.'

Cobain's fate was to be hailed as the spokesman for his own story, a status with which he was very uncomfortable. There are few dates on the reproduced pages of his diary, but at one point he writes 'I really haven't had that exciting of a life. There are a lot of things I wish I would have done, instead of just sitting around and complaining about having a boring life. So I pretty much like to make it up. I'd rather tell a story about somebody else.' His diaries contain first drafts of many of his songs.

Like so many other members of the "27 Club" – Jimi Hendrix, Jani Joplin, Jim Morrison and Amy Winehouse among them – the endless cycle of recording, promoting and touring took its toll on Kurt Cobain, and he used readily available drugs to deal with physical and mental fatigue which damaged him. A page from one of his later notebooks reads like a string of unconnected ideas. Yet there is a sense of rhythm and repetition which clearly lends itself to the composition of song lyrics: 'The king of words is EVERY thing. I can only fuck and sing. Have you ever felt like you cared so much that you wanted to kill [the word "everything" is scribbled out] your germs? Who will be the King and Queen of the outcasts? I've lost my MIND many times and my wallet many more.'

Readers wonder whether he is writing lyrics, or merely his fast-flashing thoughts in the diary. The same page concludes with advice for the ages. 'In simplest terms: 1. Don't rape. 2. Don't be prejudice [sic]. 3. Don't be sexist. 4. Love your children. 5. Love your neighbor. 6. Love yourself. Don't let your opinions obstruct the afore mentioned list.'

ABOVE: Kurt Cobain performing at a concert in 1993. Nirvana sold more than 75 million records worldwide, as well as receiving countless awards.

ABOVE: Columbine High School was the site of an infamous massacre in April 1999. It was the deadliest single mass school shooting in US history, until 2007.

Eric Harris and Dylan Klebold, perpetrators of the Columbine High School massacre

(1981–1999)

The mass shooting of children and teachers is a sad strand of modern history. The two American boys who committed the Columbine High School massacre in 1999 both kept lengthy journals in which they vented their teenage fury and outlined their heinous plans.

Harris was eleven days over eighteen and Klebold seven months under when they killed thirteen pupils and staff and injured twenty-four others, before turning their weapons on themselves.

The pair were inseparable in High School. They did have a few friends, but generally sat apart, for which they were teased. Harris was from a US Air Force family and had moved around a lot before settling in Columbine, Colorado. He was full of anger at having had to leave friends behind so often. Klebold was born in Colorado; he was introverted and depressive. Where Harris was quick to anger, Klebold would bottle his emotions until they exploded out of him. It is believed that shy Klebold was attracted to the unrestrained psychopathy of Harris.

Klebold began keeping a journal of his feelings in March 1997, two years before the attack and Harris started his own a year later. His first entry, in April 1998, is almost a parody of disenchanted youth. It reads: 'I hate the fucking world, too much god damn fuckers in it. Too many thoughts and different societies all wrapped up together in this fucking place called AMERICA. Everyone has their own god damn opinions on every god damn thing and you may be saying "well what makes you so different?" because I have something only me and Vodka have, SELF AWARENESS.'

Vodka was a nickname Klebold chose for himself. His own first entry is much more inward-looking than Harris's. 'Ah yes, this is me writing ... this is a weird time, weird life, weird existence. As I sit here (partially drunk with a screwdriver) I think a lot. Think ... think ... that's all my life is, just shitloads of thinking ... all the time ... my mind never stops ... music runs 24/7 (except for sleep), just songs I hear, not necessarily good or bad, & thinking ... about the asshole in gym class, how he worries me, about driving, & my family, about friends & doings with them, about girls I know (mainly &) how I know I can never have them, yet I can still dream ...' Still concerned about his human relationships at this early stage, Klebold eventually became the more detached from reality of the two.

The pair were influenced by films, especially in portrayals of extreme violence such as zombie movies. The last entry in Harris's diary is chillingly practical. 'We test fired all of our babies, we have 6 time clocks ready, 39 crickets [small bombs], 24 pipe bombs, and the napalm is under construction. ... Everything I see and hear I incorporate into NBK.' NBK was the boys' codeword for the coming massacre - it stood for the mass-murderer movie *Natural Born Killers*. 'Feels like a goddamn movie sometimes..'

At the end of the entry, his thoughts turn again to hurt and hate: 'I hate you people for leaving me out of so many fun things. And no don't fucking say "well that's your fault" because it isn't, you people had my phone #, and I asked and all, but no no no no don't let the weird looking Eric KID come along, ooh fucking nooo.'

Klebold eventually developed a god-complex, and his last written words are: 'What fun is life without a little death?' It was as if he had completely separated his mind from his body. 'It's interesting, when I'm in my human form, knowing I'm going to die. ... In 26.4 hours I'll be dead, & in happiness.'

Picture Credits

The publisher wishes to credit the following sources for the images on the following pages:

Alamy: 6, 9, 10, 11, 12, 13, 14, 17, 22, 25, 26, 29, 30, 33, 34, 37 (both images), 38, 45, 46, 49, 50, 53, 57, 73, 78, 86, 89, 90, 94, 97, 106, 109, 110, 113, 120 (top), 124 (both images), 127, 128, 136, 148, 155, 159, 160, 168, 171, 172, 175, 176, 179, 180, 183, 184, 188, 191, 192, 195, 199, 200, 204, 211, 217, 218

Arquivo Nacional Collection, Brazil/Wikimedia Commons: 187

Bridgeman Images: 74

Calderdale Metropolitan Borough Council/Wikimedia Commons: 85

Carl Van Vechten Photographs, Library of Congress/Wikimedia Commons: 167

Getty Images: 156, 203, 207, 208, 212

Houghton Library, Harvard University/Wikimedia Commons: 18

Howard University/Wikimedia Commons: 116

Mair Owen and Brian Jenkins/Wikimedia Commons: 101

Mitchell Library, State Library of New South Wales/Wikimedia Commons: 66

National Archives Catalog/Wikimedia Commons: 147

National Gallery of Ireland/Wikimedia Commons: 135

National Library of Wales/Wikimedia Commons: 58

National Maritime Museum, London/Wikimedia Commons: 41

National Portrait Gallery, London: 65, 98

New York Public Library/Wikimedia Commons: 123

Newstead Abbey Collection/Wikimedia Commons: 81

Royal Collection Trust/Wikimedia Commons: 139

Shutterstock: 2-3, 21, 36, 54, 69, 70, 77, 82, 93, 102, 144, 164, 196, 221, 222

The Colonial Williamsburg Foundation/Wikimedia Commons: 42, 62

Tretyakov Gallery/Wikimedia Commons: 105

United States Capitol/Wikimedia Commons: 61

University of Aberdeen: 120 (bottom)

Wikimedia Commons: 114, 119, 131, 132, 140, 143, 151, 152, 163

Every effort has been made to credit the material used in this book. If your material has not been credited, please contact us and we will update this in future editions.

Index

OPPOSITE: *What is believed to be the last image of Che Guevara and the final page from his journal.*

LEFT: Often considered the most famous diary in the world: Anne Frank's story.

RIGHT: A portrait of Queen Victoria, whose diaries offer an incredible account of the events of her reign.

LEFT: Courtney Love made the controversial decision to publish her late husband's letters and diaries after his death in 1994.

Acknowledgements

I would like to thank all diary writers, especially those who write them in longhand. In a world of electronic record-keeping, it only takes one power failure or a carelessly pressed 'delete' button to wipe out vital memories of lives lived today and yesterday.

Thank-you to the school nurse who gave me my first diary at the age of seventeen. I've forgotten her name, but I still have the diary.

Thanks to Frank Hopkinson, my editor and publisher for many years, for commissioning this latest addition to the "100s" series; and to Shamar Gunning at Pavilion Books for guiding it from my rough drafts to the present smart volume.

Special thanks to my wife Rosemary Doyle, whose arrival in my life caused me to stop writing a diary altogether for a time, so distracted by her was I. She has taught me the value of journalling, not only to remember the past but to order my thoughts for the future.

Also in this series:

100 Children's Books That Inspire Our World ISBN: 978-1-911641-08-7
Colin Salter (2020)

100 Posters That Changed the World ISBN: 978-1-911641-45-2
Colin Salter (2020)

100 Science Discoveries That Changed the World ISBN: 978-1-911663-54-6
Colin Salter (2021)

100 Symbols That Changed the World ISBN: 978-1-911216-38-4
Colin Salter (2022)

100 Novels That Changed the World ISBN: 978-0-00-859908-9
Colin Salter (2023)

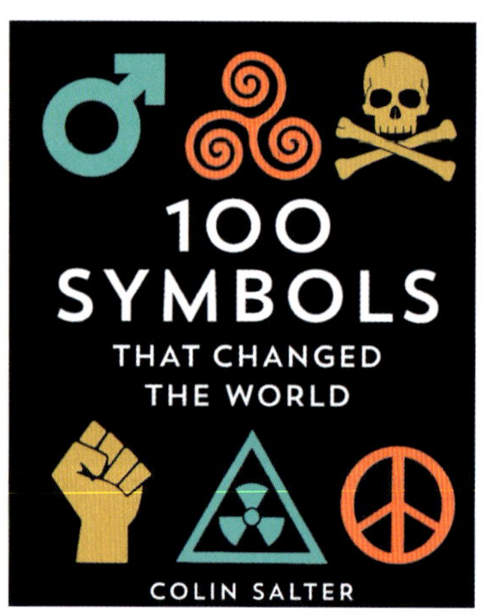

About the Author

Colin Salter is the author of nine books in Pavilion's *100s* series, each telling the history of the world as recorded by humankind's use of words in books, speeches, letters and now diaries. His latest book *The History Trees* takes a different perspective on history, as seen through its silent witnesses – the trees which have lived through major human events. Colin also writes on science history, most recently in *The Anatomists' Library* (Quarto), and on travel, notably in his trilogy of *Remarkable Road Trips*, *Bicycle Rides* and *Treks* (Pavilion). Colin has kept a diary since the age of sixteen.